THE BALCONY

by the same author

*

THE MAIDS
THE BLACKS: A CLOWN SHOW
DEATHWATCH
REFLECTIONS ON THE THEATRE
FUNERAL RITES
MIRACLE OF THE ROSES
OUR LADY OF THE FLOWERS
QUERELLE OF BREST
THE THIEF'S JOURNAL

THE BALCONY

by

JEAN GENET

translated by

BERNARD FRECHTMAN

Revised Version

FABER AND FABER

3 Queen Square

London

First published in 1958
by Faber and Faber Limited
3 Queen Square London WC1
First Published in Faber Paper Covered Editions 1965
Second edition (revised) 1966
Reprinted 1971 and 1975
Printed in Great Britain by
Whitstable Litho Ltd., Whitstable, Kent
All rights reserved

ISBN 0 571 04595 2

This play is a translation of
LE BALCON (revised edition, 1962)

CHARACTERS

THE BISHOP
THE JUDGE
THE EXECUTIONER (ARTHUR)
THE GENERAL
THE CHIEF OF POLICE
THE BEGGAR
ROGER
THE COURT ENVOY
THE FIRST PHOTOGRAPHER
THE SECOND PHOTOGRAPHER
THE THIRD PHOTOGRAPHER
IRMA (THE QUEEN)
THE WOMAN (ROSINE)
THE THIEF
THE GIRL
CARMEN
CHANTAL

SCENE ONE

On the ceiling, a chandelier, which will remain the same in each scene. The set seems to represent a sacristy, formed by three blood-red, cloth folding-screens. The one at the rear has a built-in door. Above, a huge Spanish crucifix, drawn in trompe l'oeil. *On the right wall, a mirror, with a carved gilt frame, reflects an unmade bed which, if the room were arranged logically, would be in the first rows of the orchestra. A table with a large jug. A yellow armchair. On the chair, a pair of black trousers, a shirt and a jacket.* THE BISHOP, *in mitre and gilded cope, is sitting in the chair. He is obviously larger than life. The role is played by an actor wearing tragedian's cothurni about twenty inches high. His shoulders, on which the cope lies, are inordinately broadened so that when the curtain rises he looks huge and stiff, like a scarecrow. He wears garish make-up. At the side, a woman, rather young, highly made up and wearing a lace dressing-gown, is drying her hands with a towel. Standing by is another woman,* IRMA. *She is about forty, dark, severe-looking, and is wearing a black tailored suit and a hat with a tight string (like a chin-strap).*

THE BISHOP (*sitting in the chair, middle of the stage. In a low but fervent voice*): In truth, the mark of a prelate is not mildness or unction, but the most rigorous intelligence. Our heart is our undoing. We think we are master of our kindness; we are the slaves of a serene laxity. It is something quite other than intelligence that is involved. . . . (*He hesitates.*) It may be cruelty. And beyond that cruelty—and through it—a skilful, vigorous course towards Absence. Towards Death. God? (*Smiling*) I can read your mind! (*To his mitre*) Mitre, bishop's bonnet, when my eyes close for the last time, it is you that I shall see behind my eyelids, you, my beautiful gilded hat . . . you, my handsome ornaments, copes, laces. . . .

7

IRMA (*bluntly*): An agreement's an agreement. When a deal's been made. . . .

(*Throughout the scene she hardly moves. She is standing very near the door.*)

THE BISHOP (*very gently, waving her aside with a gesture*): And when the die is cast. . . .

IRMA: No. Twenty. Twenty and no nonsense. Or I'll lose my temper. And that's not like me. . . . Now, if you have any difficulties. . . .

THE BISHOP (*curtly, and tossing away the mitre*): Thank you.

IRMA: And don't break anything. We need that. (*To the woman*) Put it away.

(*She lays the mitre on the table, near the jug.*)

THE BISHOP (*after a deep sigh*): I've been told that this house is going to be besieged. The rebels have already crossed the river.

IRMA: There's blood everywhere. . . . You can slip round behind the Archbishop's Palace. Then, down Fishmarket Street. . . .

(*Suddenly a scream of pain, uttered by a woman off-stage.*)

IRMA (*annoyed*): But I told them to be quiet. Good thing I remembered to cover the windows with padded curtains. (*Suddenly amiable, insidious*)

Well, and what was it this evening? A blessing? A prayer? A mass? A perpetual adoration?

THE BISHOP (*gravely*): Let's not talk about that now. It's over. I'm concerned only about getting home. . . . You say the city's splashed with blood. . . .

THE WOMAN: There was a blessing, Madame. Then, my confession. . . .

IRMA: And after that?

THE BISHOP: That'll do!

THE WOMAN: That was all. At the end, my absolution.

IRMA: Won't anyone be able to witness it? Just once?

THE BISHOP (*frightened*): No, no. Those things must remain secret, and they shall. It's indecent enough to talk about them while I'm being undressed. Nobody. And all the doors

8

must be closed. Firmly closed, shut, buttoned, laced, hooked, sewn. . . .

IRMA: I merely asked. . . .

THE BISHOP: Sewn, Madame.

IRMA (*annoyed*): You'll allow me at least, won't you, to feel a little uneasy . . . professionally? I said twenty.

THE BISHOP (*his voice suddenly grows clear and sharp, as if he were awakening. He displays a little annoyance*): We didn't tire ourselves. Barely six sins, and far from my favourite ones.

THE WOMAN: Six, but deadly ones! And it was a job finding *those*.

THE BISHOP (*uneasy*): What? You mean they were false?

THE WOMAN: They were real, all right! I mean it was a job committing them. If only you realized what it takes, what a person has to go through, in order to reach the point of disobedience.

THE BISHOP: I can imagine, my child. The order of the world is so lax that you can do as you please there—or almost. But if your sins were false, you may say so now.

IRMA: Oh no! I can hear you complaining already the next time you come. No. They were real. (*To the woman*) Untie his laces. Take off his shoes. And when you dress him, be careful he doesn't catch cold. (*To the Bishop*) Would you like a toddy, a hot drink?

THE BISHOP: Thank you. I haven't time. I must be going. (*Dreamily*)
Yes, six, but deadly ones!

IRMA: Come here, we'll undress you!

THE BISHOP (*pleading, almost on his knees*): No, no, not yet.

IRMA: It's time. Come on! Quick! Make it snappy!
(*While they talk, the women undress him. Or rather they merely remove pins and untie cords that seem to secure the cope, stole and surplice.*)

THE BISHOP (*to the woman*): About the sins, you really did commit them?

THE WOMAN: I did.

THE BISHOP: You really made the gestures? All the gestures?

9

THE WOMAN: I did.

THE BISHOP: When you moved towards me with your face forward, was it really aglow with the light of the flames?

THE WOMAN: It was.

THE BISHOP: And when my ringed hand came down on your forehead, forgiving it. . . .

THE WOMAN: It was.

THE BISHOP: And when my gaze pierced your lovely eyes?

THE WOMAN: It was.

IRMA: Was there at least a glimmer of repentance in her lovely eyes, my Lord?

THE BISHOP (*standing up*): A fleeting glimmer. But was I seeking repentance in them? I saw there the greedy longing for transgression. In flooding it, evil all at once baptized it. Her big eyes opened on the abyss . . . a deathly pallor lit up— yes, Madame—lit up her face. But our holiness lies only in our being able to forgive you your sins. Even if they're only make-believe.

THE WOMAN (*suddenly coy*): And what if my sins were real?

THE BISHOP (*in a different, less theatrical tone*): You're mad! I hope you really didn't do all that!

IRMA (*to the Bishop*): Don't listen to her. As for her sins, don't worry. Here there's no. . . .

THE BISHOP (*interrupting her*): I'm quite aware of that. Here there's no possibility of doing evil. You live in evil. In the absence of remorse. How could you do evil? The Devil makes believe. That's how one recognizes him. He's the great Actor. And that's why the Church has anathematized actors.

THE WOMAN: Reality frightens you, doesn't it?

THE BISHOP: If your sins were real, they would be crimes, and I'd be in a fine mess.

THE WOMAN: Would you go to the police?

(IRMA *continues to undress him. However, he still has the cope on his shoulders.*)

IRMA: Stop plaguing her with all those questions.

(*The same terrible scream is heard again.*)

They're at it again! I'll go and shut them up.

THE BISHOP: That wasn't a make-believe scream.

IRMA (*anxiously*): I don't know. . . . Who knows and what does it matter?

THE BISHOP (*going slowly to the mirror. He stands in front of it*): Now answer, mirror, answer me. Do I come here to discover evil and innocence? (*To Irma, very gently*) Leave the room! I want to be by myself.

IRMA: It's late. And the later it gets, the more dangerous it'll be . . .

THE BISHOP (*pleading*): Just one more minute.

IRMA: You've been here two hours and twenty minutes. In other words, twenty minutes too long. . . .

THE BISHOP (*suddenly incensed*): I want to be by myself. Eavesdrop, if you want to—I know you do, anyway—and don't come back till I've finished.

(*The two women leave with a sigh, looking as if they were out of patience. The Bishop remains alone.*)

THE BISHOP (*after making a visible effort to calm himself, in front of the mirror and holding his surplice*): Now answer, mirror, answer me. Do I come here to discover evil and innocence? And in your gilt-edged glass, what was I? Never—I affirm it before God Who sees me—I never desired the episcopal throne. To become bishop, to work my way up—by means of virtues or vices—would have been to turn away from the ultimate dignity of bishop. I shall explain: (THE BISHOP *speaks in a tone of great precision, as if pursuing a line of logical reasoning*) in order to become a bishop, I should have had to make a zealous effort not to be one, but to do what would have resulted in my being one. Having become a bishop, in order to be one I should have had—in order to be one for myself, of course!—I should have had to be constantly aware of being one so as to perform my function. (*He seizes the flap of his surplice and kisses it.*) Oh laces, laces, fashioned by a thousand little hands to veil ever so many panting bosoms, buxom bosoms, and faces, and hair, you illustrate me with branches and flowers! Let us continue. But—there's the crux!

(*He laughs.*)

11

So I speak Latin!—a function is a function. It's not a mode of being. But a bishop—that's a mode of being. It's a trust. A burden. Mitres, lace, gold-cloth and glass trinkets, genuflexions. . . . To hell with the function!

(*Crackling of machine-gun fire.*)

IRMA (*putting her head through the door*): Have you finished?

THE BISHOP: For Christ's sake, leave me alone. Get the hell out! I'm probing myself.

(IRMA *shuts the door.*)

THE BISHOP (*to the mirror*): The majesty, the dignity, that light up my person, do not emanate from the attributions of my function.—No more, good heavens! than from my personal merits.—The majesty, the dignity that light me up come from a more mysterious brilliance: the fact that the bishop precedes me. Do I make myself clear, mirror, gilded image, ornate as a box of Mexican cigars? And I wish to be bishop in solitude, for appearance alone. . . . And in order to destroy all function, I want to cause a scandal and feel you up, you slut, you bitch, you trollop, you tramp. . . .

IRMA (*entering*): That'll do now. You've got to leave.

THE BISHOP: You're crazy! I haven't finished.

(*Both women have entered.*)

IRMA: I'm not trying to pick an argument, and you know it, but you've no time to waste. . . .

THE BISHOP (*ironically*): What you mean is that you need the room for someone else and you've got to arrange the mirrors and jugs.

IRMA (*very irritated*): That's no business of yours. I've given you every attention while you've been here. And I repeat that it's dangerous for anyone to loiter in the streets.

(*Sound of gun-fire in the distance.*)

THE BISHOP (*bitterly*): That's not true. You don't give a damn about my safety. When the job's finished, you don't give a damn about anyone!

IRMA (*to the girl*): Stop listening to him and undress him.

IRMA (*to the Bishop, who has stepped down from his cothurni and has now assumed the normal size of an actor, of the most ordinary of actors*): Lend a hand. You're stiff.

12

THE BISHOP (*with a foolish look*): Stiff? I'm stiff? A solemn
    stiffness! Final immobility. . . .

IRMA (*to the girl*): Hand him his jacket. . . .

THE BISHOP (*looking at his clothes, which are heaped on the floor*):
    Ornaments, laces, through you I re-enter myself. I
    reconquer a domain. I beleaguer a very ancient place from
    which I was driven. I install myself in a clearing where
    suicide at last becomes possible. The judgment depends on
    me, and here I stand, face to face with my death.

IRMA: That's all very fine, but you've got to go. You left your
    car at the front door, near the power-station.

THE BISHOP (*to Irma*): Because our Chief of Police, that wretched
    incompetent, is letting us be slaughtered by the rabble!
    (*Turning to the mirror and declaiming*) Ornaments! Mitres!
    Laces! You, above all, oh gilded cope, you protect me from
    the world. Where are my legs, where are my arms? Under
    your scalloped, lustrous flaps, what have my hands been
    doing? Fit only for fluttering gestures, they've become mere
    stumps of wings—not of angels, but of partridges!—rigid
    cope, you make it possible for the most tender and
    luminous sweetness to ripen in warmth and darkness. My
    charity, a charity that will flood the world—it was under
    this carapace that I distilled it. . . . Would my hand emerge
    at times, knife-like, to bless? Or cut, mow down? My hand,
    the head of a turtle, would push aside the flaps. A turtle or
    a cautious snake? And go back into the rock. Underneath,
    my hand would dream. . . . Ornaments, gilded copes. . . .
    (*The stage moves from left to right, as if it were plunging into
    the wings. The following set then appears.*)

SCENE TWO

*Same chandelier. Three brown folding-screens. Bare walls. At
right, same mirror, in which is reflected the same unmade bed as in
the first scene. A woman, young and beautiful, seems to be chained,
with her wrists bound. Her muslin dress is torn. Her breasts are*

13

visible. Standing in front of her is the executioner. He is a giant, stripped to the waist. Very muscular. His whip has been slipped through the loop of his belt, in back, so that he seems to have a tail. A JUDGE, *who, when he stands up, will seem larger than life (he, too, is mounted on cothurni, which are invisible beneath his robe, and his face is made up) is crawling, on his stomach, towards the woman, who shrinks as he approaches.*

THE THIEF (*holding out her foot*): Not yet! Lick it! Lick it first. . . .
   (THE JUDGE *makes an effort to continue crawling. Then he stands up and, slowly and painfully, though apparently happy, goes and sits down on a stool.* THE THIEF (*the woman described above*) *drops her domineering attitude and becomes humble.*)
THE JUDGE (*severely*): For you're a thief! You were caught. . . . Who? The police. . . . Have you forgotten that your movements are hedged about by a strong and subtle network, my strong-arm cops? They're watchful, swivel-eyed insects that lie in wait for you. All of you! And they bring you captive, all of you, to the Bench. . . . What have you to say for yourself? You were caught. . . . Under your skirt. . . . (*To the Executioner.*) Put your hand under her skirt. You'll find the pocket, the notorious Kangaroo Pocket. . . . (*To the Thief*) that you fill with any old junk you pick up. Because you're an idiot to boot. . . . (*To the Executioner.*) What was there in that notorious Kangaroo Pocket? In that enormous paunch?
THE EXECUTIONER: Bottles of scent, my Lord, a flashlight, a bottle of Fly-tox, some oranges, several pairs of socks, bearskins, a Turkish towel, a scarf. (*To the Judge.*) Do you hear me? I said: a scarf.
THE JUDGE (*with a start*): A scarf? Ah ha, so that's it? Why the scarf? Eh? What were you going to do with it? Whom were you planning to strangle? Answer. Who? . . . Are you a thief or a strangler? (*Very gently, imploringly*) Tell me, my child, I beg of you, tell me you're a thief.
THE THIEF: Yes, my Lord.

14

THE EXECUTIONER: No!

THE THIEF (*looking at him in surprise*): No?

THE EXECUTIONER: That's for later.

THE THIEF: Eh?

THE EXECUTIONER: I mean the confession is supposed to come later. Plead not guilty.

THE THIEF: What, and get beaten again!

THE JUDGE (*mealy-mouthed*): Exactly, my child: and get beaten. You must first deny, then admit and repent. I want to see hot tears gush from your lovely eyes. Oh! I want you to be drenched in them. The power of tears! . . . Where's my statute-book? (*He fishes under his robe and pulls out a book.*)

THE THIEF: I've already cried. . . .

THE JUDGE (*he seems to be reading*): Under the blows. I want tears of repentance. When I see you wet as a meadow I'll be utterly satisfied!

THE THIEF: It's not easy. I tried to cry before. . . .

THE JUDGE (*no longer reading. In a half-theatrical, almost familiar tone*): You're quite young. Are you new here? (*Anxiously*) At least you're not a minor?

THE THIEF: Oh no, sir.

THE JUDGE: Call me my Lord. How long have you been here?

THE EXECUTIONER: Since the day before yesterday, my Lord.

THE JUDGE (*reassuming the theatrical tone and resuming the reading*): Let her speak. I like that puling voice of hers, that voice without resonance. . . . Look here: you've got to be a model thief if I'm to be a model judge. If you're a fake thief, I become a fake judge. Is that clear?

THE THIEF: Oh yes, my Lord.

THE JUDGE (*he continues reading*): Good. Thus far everything has gone off well. My executioner has hit hard . . . for he too has his function. We are bound together, you, he and I. For example, if he didn't hit, how could I stop him from hitting? Therefore, he must strike so that I can intervene and demonstrate my authority. And you must deny your guilt so that he can beat you.

(*A noise is heard, as of something having fallen in the next room. In a natural tone*)

15

What's that? Are all the doors firmly shut? Can anyone see us, or hear us?

THE EXECUTIONER: No, no, you needn't worry. I bolted the door. (*He goes to examine a huge bolt on the rear door.*)
And the corridor's out of bounds.

THE JUDGE (*in a natural tone*): Are you sure?

THE EXECUTIONER: You can take my word for it. (*He puts his hand into his pocket.*)
Can I have a smoke?

THE JUDGE (*in a natural tone*): The smell of tobacco inspires me. Smoke away.
(*Same noise as before.*)
Oh, what *is* that? What *is* it? Can't they leave me in peace? (*He gets up.*)
What's going on?

THE EXECUTIONER (*curtly*): Nothing at all. Someone must have dropped something. You're getting nervous.

THE JUDGE (*in a natural tone*): That may be, but my nervousness makes me aware of things. It keeps me on the alert. (*He gets up and moves towards the wall.*)
May I have a look?

THE EXECUTIONER: Just a quick one, because it's getting late. (THE EXECUTIONER *shrugs his shoulders and exchanges a wink with the thief.*)

THE JUDGE (*after looking*): It's lit up. Brightly lit, but empty.

THE EXECUTIONER (*shrugging his shoulders*): Empty!

THE JUDGE (*in an even more familiar tone*): You seem anxious. Has anything new happened?

THE EXECUTIONER: This afternoon, just before you arrived, the rebels took three key-positions. They set fire to several places. Not a single fireman came out. Everything went up in flames. The Palace. . . .

THE JUDGE: What about the Chief of Police? Twiddling his thumbs as usual?

THE THIEF: There's been no news of him for four hours. If he can get away, he's sure to come here. He's expected at any moment.

THE JUDGE (*to the Thief, and sitting down*): In any case, he'd better not plan to come by way of Queen's Bridge. It was blown up last night.

THE THIEF: We know that. We heard the explosion from here.

THE JUDGE (*resuming his theatrical tone. He reads the statute-book*): All right. Let's get on with it. Thus, taking advantage of the sleep of the just, taking advantage of a moment's inattention, you rob them, you ransack, you pilfer and purloin. . . .

THE THIEF: No, my Lord, never. . . .

THE EXECUTIONER: Shall I tan her hide?

THE THIEF (*crying out*): Arthur!

THE EXECUTIONER: What's eating you? Don't address me. Answer his Lordship. And call me Mr. Executioner.

THE THIEF: Yes, Mr. Executioner.

THE JUDGE (*reading*): I continue: did you steal?

THE THIEF: I did, I did, my Lord.

THE JUDGE (*reading*): Good. Now answer quickly, and to the point: what else did you steal?

THE THIEF: Bread, because I was hungry.

THE JUDGE (*he draws himself up and lays down the book*): Sublime! Sublime function! I'll have all that to judge. Oh, child, you reconcile me with the world. A judge! I'm going to be judge of your acts! On me depends the weighing, the balance. The world is an apple. I cut it in two: the good, the bad. And you agree, thank you, you agree to be the bad! (*Facing the audience*) Right before your eyes: nothing in my hands, nothing up my sleeve, remove the rot and cast it off. But it's a painful occupation. If every judgment were delivered seriously, each one would cost me my life. That's why I'm dead. I inhabit that region of exact freedom. I, King of Hell, weigh those who are dead, like me. She's a dead person, like myself.

THE THIEF: You frighten me, sir.

THE JUDGE (*very bombastically*): Be still. In the depths of Hell I sort out the humans who venture there. Some to the flames, the others to the boredom of the fields of asphodel. You, thief, spy, she-dog, Minos is speaking to you, Minos weighs you. (*To the Executioner*) Cerberus?

17

THE EXECUTIONER (*imitating the dog*): Bow-wow, bow-wow!

THE JUDGE: You're handsome! And the sight of a fresh victim makes you even handsomer. (*He curls up the Executioner's lips.*) Show your fangs. Dreadful. White. (*Suddenly he seems anxious. To the Thief*) But at least you're not lying about those thefts—you did commit them, didn't you?

THE EXECUTIONER: Don't worry. She committed them, all right. She wouldn't have dared not to. I'd have made her.

THE JUDGE: I'm almost happy. Continue. What did you steal? (*Suddenly, machine-gun fire.*)

THE JUDGE: There's simply no end to it. Not a moment's rest.

THE THIEF: I told you: the rebellion has spread all over the north of the city. . . .

THE EXECUTIONER: Shut up!

THE JUDGE (*irritated*): Are you going to answer, yes or no? What else have you stolen? Where? When? How? How much? Why? For whom?

THE THIEF: I very often entered houses when the maids were off. I used the tradesmen's entrance. . . . I stole from drawers, I broke into children's piggy-banks. (*She is visibly trying to find words.*)
Once I dressed up as a lady. I put on a dark-brown suit, a black straw hat with cherries, a veil and a pair of black shoes—with Cuban heels—then I went in. . . .

THE JUDGE (*in a rush*): Where? Where? Where? Where—where—where? Where did you go in?

THE THIEF: I can't remember. Forgive me.

THE EXECUTIONER: Shall I let her have it?

THE JUDGE: Not yet. (*To the girl*) Where did you go in? Tell me where?

THE THIEF (*in a panic*): But I swear to you, I don't remember.

THE EXECUTIONER: Shall I let her have it? Shall I, my Lord?

THE JUDGE (*to the Executioner, and going up to him*): Ah! ah! your pleasure depends on me. You like to thrash, eh? I'm pleased with you, Executioner! Masterly mountain of meat, hunk of beef that's set in motion at a word from me! (*He pretends to look at himself in the Executioner.*) Mirror that glorifies me! Image that I can touch, I love

18

you. Never would I have the strength or skill to leave streaks of fire on her back. Besides, what could I do with such strength and skill? (*He touches him.*) Are you there? You're all there, my huge arm, too heavy for me, too big, too fat for my shoulder, walking at my side all by itself! Arm, hundredweight of meat, without you I'd be nothing. . . . (*To the Thief*) And without you too, my child. You're my two perfect complements. . . . Ah, what a fine trio we make! (*To the Thief*) But you, you have a privilege that he hasn't, nor I either, that of priority. My being a judge is an emanation of your being a thief. You need only refuse— but you'd better not!—need only refuse to be who you are—what you are, therefore who you are—for me to cease to be . . . to vanish, evaporated. Burst. Volatilized. Denied. Hence: good born of. . . . What then? What then? But you won't refuse, will you? You won't refuse to be a thief? That would be wicked. It would be criminal. You'd deprive me of being! (*Imploringly*) Say it, my child, my love, you won't refuse?

THE THIEF (*coyly*): I might.

THE JUDGE: What's that? What's that you say? You'd refuse? Tell me where. And tell me again what you've stolen.

THE THIEF (*curtly, and getting up*): I won't.

THE JUDGE: Tell me where. Don't be cruel. . . .

THE THIEF: Your tone is getting too familiar. I won't have it!

THE JUDGE: Miss. . . . Madame. I beg of you. (*He falls to his knees.*) Look, I beseech you. Don't leave me in this position, waiting to be a judge. If there were no judge, what would become of us, but what if there were no thieves?

THE THIEF (*ironically*): And what if there weren't?

THE JUDGE: It would be awful. But you won't do that to me, will you? Please understand me: I don't mind your hiding, for as long as you can and as long as my nerves can bear it, behind the refusal to confess—it's all right to be mean and make me yearn, even prance, make me dance, drool, sweat, whinny with impatience, crawl . . . do you want me to crawl?

THE EXECUTIONER (*to the Judge*): Crawl.

THE JUDGE: I'm proud!

THE EXECUTIONER (*threateningly*): Crawl!

(THE JUDGE, *who was on his knees, lies flat on his stomach and crawls slowly towards the Thief. As he crawls forward, the Thief moves back.*)

THE EXECUTIONER: Good. Continue.

THE JUDGE (*to the Thief*): You're quite right, you rascal, to make me crawl after my judgeship, but if you were to refuse for good, you hussy, it would be criminal. . . .

THE THIEF (*haughtily*): Call me Madame, and ask politely.

THE JUDGE: Will I get what I want?

THE THIEF (*coyly*): It costs a lot—stealing does.

THE JUDGE: I'll pay! I'll pay whatever I have to, Madame. But if I no longer had to divide the Good from the Evil, of what use would I be? I ask you?

THE THIEF: I ask myself.

THE JUDGE (*is infinitely sad*): A while ago I was going to be Minos. My Cerberus was barking. (*To the Executioner*) Do you remember? (THE EXECUTIONER *interrupts the Judge by cracking his whip.*) You were so cruel, so mean! So good! And me, I was pitiless. I was going to fill Hell with the souls of the damned, to fill prisons. Prisons! Prisons! Prisons, dungeons, blessed places where evil is impossible since they are the crossroads of all the malediction in the world. One cannot commit evil in evil. Now, what I desire above all is not to condemn, but to judge. . . . (*He tries to get up.*)

THE EXECUTIONER: Crawl! And hurry up, I've got to go and get dressed.

THE JUDGE (*to the girl*): Madame! Madame, please, I beg of you. I'm willing to lick your shoes, but tell me you're a thief. . . .

THE THIEF (*in a cry*): Not yet! Lick! Lick! Lick first!

(*The stage moves from left to right, as at the end of the preceding scene, and plunges into the right wing. In the distance, machine-gun fire.*)

SCENE THREE

Three dark-green folding-screens, arranged as in the preceding scenes. The same chandelier. The same mirror reflecting the unmade bed. On an armchair, a horse of the kind used by folk-dancers, with a little kilted skirt. In the room, a timid-looking gentleman: the GENERAL. *He removes his jacket, then his bowler hat and his gloves.* IRMA *is near him.*

THE GENERAL (*He points to the hat, jacket and gloves*): Have that cleared out.

IRMA: It'll be folded and wrapped.

THE GENERAL: Have it removed from sight.

IRMA: It'll be put away. Even burned.

THE GENERAL: Yes, yes, of course, I'd like it to burn! Like cities at twilight.

IRMA: Did you notice anything on the way?

THE GENERAL: I ran very serious risks. The populace has blown up dams. Whole areas are flooded. The arsenal in particular. So that all the powder supplies are wet. And the weapons rusty. I had to make some rather wide detours—though I didn't trip over a single drowned body.

IRMA: I wouldn't take the liberty of asking you your opinions. Everyone is free, and I'm not concerned with politics.

THE GENERAL: Then let's talk of something else. The important thing is how I'm going to get out of this place. It'll be late by the time I leave. . . .

IRMA: About it's being late. . . .

THE GENERAL: That does it.

(*He reaches into his pocket, takes out some banknotes, counts them and gives some to Irma. She keeps them in her hand.*)

THE GENERAL: I'm not keen about being shot down in the dark when I leave. For, of course, there won't be anyone to escort me?

21

IRMA: I'm afraid not. Unfortunately Arthur's not free. (*A long pause.*)

THE GENERAL (*suddenly impatient*): But . . . isn't she coming?

IRMA: I can't imagine what she's doing. I gave instructions that everything was to be ready by the time you arrived. The horse is already here. . . . I'll ring.

THE GENERAL: Don't, I'll attend to that. (*He rings.*) I like to ring! Ringing's authoritative. Ah, to ring out commands.

IRMA: In a little while, General. Oh, I'm so sorry, here am I giving you your rank. . . . In a little while you'll. . . .

THE GENERAL: Sh! Don't say it.

IRMA: You have such force, such youth! such dash!

THE GENERAL: And spurs. Will I have spurs? I said they were to be fixed to my boots. Oxblood boots, right?

IRMA: Yes, General. And patent-leather.

THE GENERAL: Oxblood. Patent-leather, very well, but with mud?

IRMA: With mud and perhaps a little blood. I've had the decorations prepared.

THE GENERAL: Authentic ones?

IRMA: Authentic ones. (*Suddenly a woman's long scream.*)

THE GENERAL: What's that?

(*He starts going to the right wall and is already bending down to look, as if there were a small crack, but* IRMA *steps in front of him.*)

IRMA: Nothing. There's always some carelessness, on both sides.

THE GENERAL: But that cry? A woman's cry. A call for help perhaps? My heart skips a beat. . . . I spring forward. . . .

IRMA (*icily*): I want no trouble here. Calm down. For the time being, you're in mufti.

THE GENERAL: That's right.

(*A woman's scream again.*)

THE GENERAL: All the same, it's disturbing. Besides, it'll be awkward.

IRMA: What on earth can she be doing?

(*She goes to ring, but by the rear door enters a very beautiful young woman, red-headed, hair undone, dishevelled. Her bosom is almost bare. She is wearing a black corset, black stockings and very high-heeled shoes. She is holding a*

22

general's uniform, complete with sword, cocked hat and boots.)

THE GENERAL (*severely*): So you finally got here? Half an hour late. That's more than's needed to lose a battle.

IRMA: She'll redeem herself, General, I know her.

THE GENERAL (*looking at the boots*): What about the blood? I don't see any blood.

IRMA: It dried. Don't forget that it's the blood of your past battles. Well, then, I'll leave you. Do you have everything you need?

THE GENERAL (*looking to the right and left*): You're forgetting. . . .

IRMA: Good God! Yes. I was forgetting.
(She lays on the chair the towels she has been carrying on her arm. Then she leaves by the rear. THE GENERAL goes to the door, then locks it. But no sooner is the door closed than someone knocks. THE GIRL goes to open it. Behind, and standing slightly back, THE EXECUTIONER, sweating, wiping himself with a towel.)

THE EXECUTIONER: Is Mme Irma here?

THE GIRL (*curtly*): In the Rose-garden. (*Correcting herself*) I'm sorry, in the Funeral Chapel.
(She closes the door.)

THE GENERAL (*irritated*): I'll be left in peace, I hope. And you're late. Where the hell were you? Didn't they give you your feed-bag? You're smiling, are you? Smiling at your rider? You recognize his hand, gentle but firm? (*He strokes her.*) My proud steed! My handsome mare, we've had many a spirited gallop together!

THE GIRL: And that's not all! I want to trip through the world with my nervous legs and well-shod hooves. Take off your trousers and shoes so I can dress you.

THE GENERAL (*he has taken the cane*): All right, but first, down on your knees! Come on, come on, bend your knees, bend them. . . .
THE GIRL *rears, utters a whinny of pleasure and kneels like a circus horse before the General.)*

THE GENERAL: Bravo! Bravo, Dove! You haven't forgotten a thing. And now, you're going to help me and answer my questions. It's fitting and proper for a nice filly to help her master unbutton himself and take off his gloves, and to be at his beck and call. Now start by untying my laces. (*During the entire scene that follows,* THE GIRL *helps* THE GENERAL *remove his clothes and then dress up as a general. When he is completely dressed, he will be seen to have taken on gigantic proportions, by means of trick effects: invisible foot-gear, broadened shoulders, excessive make-up.*)

THE GIRL: Left foot still swollen?

THE GENERAL: Yes. It's my leading-foot. The one that prances. Like your hoof when you toss your head.

THE GIRL: What am I doing? Unbutton yourself.

THE GENERAL: Are you a horse or an illiterate? If you're a horse, you toss your head. Help me. Pull. Don't pull so hard. See here, you're not a plough-horse.

THE GIRL: I do what I have to do.

THE GENERAL: Are you rebelling? Already? Wait till I'm ready. When I put the bit into your mouth. . . .

THE GIRL: Oh no, not that.

THE GENERAL: A general reprimanded by his horse! You'll have the bit, the bridle, the harness, the saddlegirth, and I, in boots and helmet, will whip and plunge!

THE GIRL: The bit is awful. It makes the gums and the corners of the lips bleed. I'll drool blood.

THE GENERAL: Foam pink and spit fire! But what a gallop! Along the rye-fields, through the alfalfa, over the meadows and dusty roads, over hill and dale, awake or asleep, from dawn to twilight and from twilight. . . .

THE GIRL: Tuck in your shirt. Pull up your braces. It's quite a job dressing a victorious general who's to be buried. Do you want the sabre?

THE GENERAL: Let it lie on the table, like Lafayette's. Conspicuously, but hide the clothes. Where? How should *I* know? Surely there's a hiding-place somewhere. (THE GIRL *bundles up his clothes and hides them behind the armchair.*)

THE GENERAL: The tunic? Good. Got all the medals? Count 'em.

THE GIRL (*after counting them, very quickly*): They're all here, sir.

THE GENERAL: What about the war? Where's the war?

THE GIRL (*very softly*): It's approaching, sir. It's evening in an apple-orchard. The sky is calm and pink. The earth is bathed in a sudden peace—the moan of doves—the peace that precedes battles. The air is very still. An apple has fallen to the grass. A yellow apple. Things are holding their breath. War is declared. The evening is very mild. . . .

THE GENERAL: But suddenly?

THE GIRL: We're at the edge of the meadow. I keep myself from flinging out, from whinnying. Your thighs are warm and you're pressing my flanks. Death. . . .

THE GENERAL: But suddenly?

THE GIRL: Death has pricked up her ears. She puts a finger to her lips, asking for silence. Things are lit up with an ultimate goodness. You yourself no longer heed my presence. . . .

THE GENERAL: But suddenly?

THE GIRL: Button up by yourself, sir. The water lay motionless in the pools. The wind itself was awaiting an order to unfurl the flags. . . .

THE GENERAL: But suddenly?

THE GIRL: Suddenly? Eh? Suddenly? (*She seems to be trying to find the right words.*) Ah yes, suddenly all was fire and sword! Widows! Miles of crêpe had to be woven to put on the standards. The mothers and wives remained dry-eyed behind their veils. The bells came clattering down the bombed towers. As I rounded a corner I was frightened by a blue cloth. I reared, but, steadied by your gentle and masterful hand, I ceased to quiver. I started forward again. How I loved you, my hero!

THE GENERAL: But . . . the dead? Weren't there any dead?

THE GIRL: The soldiers died kissing the standard. You were all victory and kindness. One evening, remember. . . .

THE GENERAL: I was so mild that I began to snow. To snow on my men, to shroud them in the softest of winding-sheets. To snow. Moskova!

HE GIRL: Splinters of shell had gashed the lemons. Now death was in action. She moved nimbly from one to the other,

25

deepening a wound, dimming an eye, tearing off an arm, opening an artery, discolouring a face, cutting short a cry, a song. Death was ready to drop. Finally, exhausted, herself dead with fatigue, she grew drowsy and rested lightly on your shoulder, where she fell asleep.

THE GENERAL (*drunk with joy*): Stop, stop, it's not time for that yet, but I feel it'll be magnificent. The cross-belt? Good. (*He looks at himself in the mirror.*) Austerlitz! General! Man of war and in full regalia, behold me in my pure appearance. Nothing, no contingent trails behind me. I appear, purely and simply. If I went through wars without dying, went through sufferings without dying, if I was promoted, without dying, it was for this minute close to death.

(*Suddenly he stops; he seems troubled by an idea.*)
Tell me, Dove?

THE GIRL: What is it, sir?

THE GENERAL: What's the Chief of Police been doing?
(THE GIRL *shakes her head.*)
Nothing? Still nothing? In short, everything slips through his fingers. And what about us, are we wasting our time?

THE GIRL (*imperiously*): Not at all. And, in any case, it's no business of ours. Continue. You were saying: for this minute close to death . . . and then?

THE GENERAL (*hesitating*): . . . close to death . . . where I shall be nothing, though reflected *ad infinitum* in these mirrors, nothing but my image. . . . Quite right, comb your mane. Curry yourself. I require a well-groomed filly. So, in a little while, to the blare of trumpets, we shall descend—I on your back—to death and glory, for I am about to die. It is indeed a descent to the grave. . . .

THE GIRL: But, sir, you've been dead since yesterday.

THE GENERAL: I know . . . but a formal and picturesque descent, by unexpected stairways. . . .

THE GIRL: You are a dead general, but an eloquent one.

THE GENERAL: Because I'm dead, prating horse. What is now speaking, and so beautifully, is Example. I am now only the image of my former self. Your turn, now. Lower your head

26

and hide your eyes, for I want to be a general in solitude.
Not even for myself, but for my image, and my image for
its image, and so on. In short, we'll be among equals.
Dove, are you ready?
(THE GIRL *nods.*)
Come now. Put on your bay dress, horse, my fine Arab steed.
(THE GENERAL *slips the mock-horse over her head. Then he
cracks his whip.*)
We're off!
(*He bows to his image in the mirror.*)
Farewell, general!
(*Then he stretches out in the arm-chair with his feet on
another chair and bows to the audience, holding himself
rigid as a corpse.* THE GIRL *places herself in front of the
chair and, on the spot, makes the movements of a horse in
motion.*)

THE GIRL: The procession has begun. . . . We're passing through
the City. . . . We're going along the river. I'm sad. . . .
The sky is overcast. The nation weeps for that splendid
hero who died in battle. . . .

THE GENERAL (starting): Dove!

THE GIRL (*turning around, in tears*): Sir?

THE GENERAL: Add that I died with my boots on!
(*He then resumes his pose.*)

THE GIRL: My hero died with his boots on! The procession
continues. Your aides-de-camp precede me. . . . Then come
I, Dove, your war-horse. . . . The military band plays a
funeral march. . . .
(*Marching in place,* THE GIRL *sings Chopin's* Funeral March,
which is continued by an invisible orchestra [*with brasses*].
Far off, machine-gun fire.)

SCENE FOUR

*A room, the three visible panels of which are three mirrors in
which is reflected a little old man, dressed as a tramp though*

27

neatly combed. He is standing motionless in the middle of the room.
Near him, looking very indifferent, a very beautiful red-haired girl.
Leather corselet, leather boots. Naked and beautiful thighs. Fur
jacket. She is waiting. So is the man. He is impatient, nervous. THE
GIRL *is motionless.*

THE MAN *removes his torn gloves tremblingly. He takes from his*
pocket a handkerchief and mops his face. He takes off his glasses,
folds them and puts them into a case, which he then slips into his
pocket.

He wipes his hands with his handkerchief.

All the gestures of the little old man are reflected in the three
mirrors.

(Three actors are needed to play the roles of the reflections.)
At length, there are three raps at the rear door.
The red-haired girl goes to the door. She says: "Yes."
The door opens a little and through the opening appear IRMA'S
hand and arm holding a whip and a very dirty and shaggy wig.

THE GIRL *takes them. The door closes.*

THE MAN'S *face lights up.*

The red-haired girl has an exaggeratedly lofty and cruel air.
She puts the wig on his head roughly.

THE MAN *takes a bouquet of artificial flowers from his pocket. He*
holds it as if he were going to offer it to the girl, who whips him and
lashes it from his hand.

THE MAN'S *face is lit up with tenderness.*

Very near-by, machine-gun fire.

THE MAN *touches his wig.*

THE MAN: What about the lice?
THE GIRL (*very coarsely*): They're there.

SCENE FIVE

IRMA'S *room. Very elegant. It is the same room that was reflected*
in the mirrors in the first three scenes. The same chandelier. Large
lace hangings suspended from the flies. Three arm-chairs. At left,

28

large window near which is an apparatus by means of which IRMA
can see what is going on in the studios. Door at right. Door at left.
IRMA *is sitting at her dressing-table, going over her accounts. Near
her, a girl:* CARMEN. *Machine-gun fire.*

CARMEN (*counting*): The bishop, twenty . . . the judge,
    twenty. . . . (*She raises her head.*) No, Madame, nothing
    yet. No Chief of Police.
IRMA (*irritated*): He's going to turn up, *if* he turns up . . . fit to
    be tied! And yet!
CARMEN: Yes, I know: it takes all kinds to make a world. But
    no Chief of Police. (*She counts again.*) The general,
    twenty . . . the sailor, twenty . . . the brat, thirty. . . .
IRMA: I've told you, Carmen, I don't like that. And I demand
    respect for the visitors. Vi-si-tors! I don't allow myself—
    my own self (*she stresses the word "own"*)—even to refer to
    them as clients. And yet! . . . (*She flashily snaps the sheaf
    of fresh banknotes that she has in her hand.*)
CARMEN (*severely; she has turned around and is glaring at* IRMA):
    For you, yes: cash and refinement.
IRMA (*trying to be conciliatory*): Those eyes! Don't be unjust.
    You've been irritable for some time now. I realize we're
    on edge because of what's going on, but things will quiet
    down. The sun will come out again. George. . . .
CARMEN: Ah, him!
IRMA: Don't sneer at the Chief of Police. If not for him we'd
    be in a fine mess. Yes, we, because you're tied up with me.
    And with him. (*A long pause.*) What disturbs me most is
    your sadness. (*Wisely.*) You've changed, Carmen. And
    even before the rebellion started. . . .
CARMEN: There's nothing much left for me to do at your
    place, Mme. Irma.
IRMA (*disconcerted*): But . . . I've put you in charge of my
    bookkeeping. You sit down at my desk and all at once my
    entire life opens out before you. I haven't a secret left, and
    you're not happy?
CARMEN: Of course, I'm grateful to you for your confidence,
    but . . . it's not the same thing.

IRMA: Do you miss "that", Carmen? (CARMEN *is silent.*) Come, come, Carmen, when you mounted the snow-covered rock with the yellow paper rose-bush—by the way, I'm going to have to store that in the cellar—and when the miraculously-healed leper swooned at the sight of you, you didn't take yourself seriously, did you, Carmen? (*Brief silence.*)

CARMEN: When our sessions are over, Madame, you never allow anyone to talk about them. So you have no idea of how we really feel. You observe it all from a distance. But if ever you once put on the dress and the blue veil, or if you were the unbuttoned penitent, or the general's mare, or the country girl tumbled in the hay. . . .

IRMA (*shocked*): Me!

CARMEN: Or the maid in a pink apron, or the archduchess deflowered by the policeman, or . . . but I'm not going to run through the whole list . . . you'd know what that does to a girl's soul, and that she's got to use a little irony in self-defence. But no, you don't even want us to talk about it among ourselves. You're afraid of a smile, of a joke.

IRMA (*very severely*): True, I don't allow any joking. A giggle, or even a smile, spoils everything. A smile means doubt. The clients want sober ceremonies. With sighs. My house is a severe place. You're allowed to play cards.

CARMEN: Then don't be surprised that we're sad. (*A pause.*) But I'm thinking of my daughter.

IRMA (*She stands—for a bell has buzzed—and goes to a curious piece of furniture at the left, a kind of switchboard with a view-finder and earphone. While talking, she looks into the view-finder, after pushing down a switch*): Every time I ask you a slightly intimate question, you shut up like a clam, and you throw your daughter up to me. Are you still set on going to see her? Don't be a fool. Between this place and the nursery in the country there's fire and water, rebellion and bullets. I even wonder whether . . . (*The bell buzzes again.* MME IRMA *pulls up the switch and pushes down another*) . . . whether they didn't get George on the way. Though a Chief of Police knows how to take care of himself. (*She looks at a watch that she takes from her*

30

bosom.) He's late. (*She looks anxious*.) Or else he hasn't dared to go out.

CARMEN: In order to get to your studios, those gentlemen of yours go through gunfire without fear, whereas I, in order to see my daughter. . . .

IRMA: Without fear? In a state of jitters that excites them. Their nostrils can sniff the orgy behind the wall of flame and steel. . . . Let's get back to the accounts, shall we?

CARMEN: In all, counting the sailor and the simple jobs, it comes to three hundred and twenty.

IRMA: The more killing there is in the working-class districts, the more the men roll into my studios.

CARMEN: The men?

IRMA (*after a pause*): Some men. Drawn by my mirrors and chandeliers, always the same ones. As for the others, heroism takes the place of women.

CARMEN (*bitterly*): Women?

IRMA: What shall I call you, my big, long, sterile girls? Their seed never ripens in you, and yet . . . if you weren't there?

CARMEN: You have your revels, Mme Irma.

IRMA: Be still. It's this chilling game that makes me sad and melancholy. Fortunately I have my jewels. Which, as it happens, are in great danger. (*Dreamily*) I have my jewels . . . and you, the orgies of your heart. . . .

CARMEN: . . . they don't help matters, Madame. My daughter loves me.

IRMA: You're the fairy godmother who comes to see her with toys and perfumes. She pictures you in Heaven. (*Bursting out laughing*) Ah, that's the limit—to think there's someone for whom my brothel—which is Hell—is Heaven! It's Heaven for your brat! (*She laughs*.) Are you going to make a whore of her later on?

CARMEN: Mme Irma!

IRMA: That's right! I ought to leave you to your secret brothel, your precious pink cat-house, your soulful whore-house. . . . You think I'm cruel? This rebellion is getting me down, too. You may not realize it, but I have moments of fear and panic. . . . It looks to me as if the aim of the rebellion weren't to capture the Royal Palace, but to sack my studios. I'm afraid, Carmen. Yet I've tried everything, even prayer. (*She smiles painfully.*) Like your miraculously-healed leper. Have I wounded you?

CARMEN (*with decision*): Twice a week, on Tuesdays and Fridays, I had to be the Immaculate Conception of Lourdes and appear to a bank-clerk of the National Provincial. For you it meant money in the bank and justified your brothel, whereas for me it was. . . .

IRMA (*astonished*): You agreed to it. You didn't seem to mind it.

CARMEN: I was happy.

IRMA: Well? Where's the harm?

CARMEN: I saw the effect I had on my bank-clerk. I saw his state of terror, how he'd break out in a sweat, I heard the rattle in his throat. . . .

IRMA: That'll do. He doesn't come any more. I wonder why? Maybe the danger. Or maybe his wife found out. (*A pause.*) Maybe he's dead. Attend to my accounts.

CARMEN: Your book-keeping will never replace my appearing to the bank-clerk. It had become as real as at Lourdes. Everything inside me now yearns for my daughter. She's in a real garden. . . .

IRMA: You'll have a hard time getting to her, and before long the garden will be in your heart.

CARMEN: Be still!

IRMA (*inexorably*): The city is full of corpses. All the roads are cut off. The peasants are also going over to the rebels. I wonder why? Contagion? The rebellion is an epidemic. It has the same fatal and sacred character. In any case, we're going to find ourselves more and more isolated. The rebels have it in for the Clergy, for the Army, for the Magistracy, for me, Irma, a bawd and madame of a whore-house. As for you, you'll be killed, disembowelled, and your daughter will be adopted by some virtuous rebel. And that's what's in store for all of us. (*She shudders.*)

(*Suddenly a buzz.* IRMA *runs to the apparatus and looks and listens as before.*)

IRMA: Studio 24, Chamber of the Sands. What's going on?
(*She watches very attentively. A long pause.*)

CARMEN (*She has sat down at Irma's table and gone back to the accounts. Without raising her head*): The Foreign Legion?

IRMA (*with her eye still glued to the apparatus*): Yes. It's the heroic Legionnaire falling to the sand. And that idiot Rachel has thrown a dart at his ear. He might have been disfigured. What an idea, having himself shot as if by an Arab, and dying—if you want to call it that!—at attention, on a sandpile! (*A silence. She watches attentively.*) Ah, Rachel's doctoring him. She's preparing a dressing for him, and he has a happy look. (*Very much interested.*) My, my, he seems to like it. I have a feeling he wants to alter his scenario and that starting today he's going to die in the military hospital, tucked in by his nurse. . . . Another uniform to buy. Always expenses. (*Suddenly anxious.*) Say, I don't like that. Not one bit. I'm getting more and more worried about Rachel. She'd better not double-cross me the way Chantal did. (*Turning around, to Carmen.*) By the way, no news of Chantal?

CARMEN: None.

IRMA (*picks up the apparatus again*): And the machine's not working right! What's he saying to her? He's explaining . . . she's listening . . . she understands. I'm afraid he understands too. (*Buzzing again. She pushes down another switch and looks.*) False alarm. It's the plumber leaving.

CARMEN: Which one?

IRMA: The real one.

CARMEN: Which is the real one?

IRMA: The one who repairs the taps.

CARMEN: Is the other one fake?

IRMA (*shrugs her shoulders and pushes down the first switch*): Ah, I told you so: the three or four drops of blood from his ear have inspired him. Now he's having her pamper him. Tomorrow morning he'll be in fine fettle for going to his Embassy.

CARMEN: He's married, isn't he?

IRMA: As a rule, I don't like to talk about the private life of my visitors. The Grand Balcony has a world-wide reputation. It's the most artful, yet the most decent house of illusions. . . .

CARMEN: Decent?

IRMA: Discreet. But I might as well be frank with you, you inquisitive girl. Most of them are married.
(*A pause.*)

CARMEN: When they're with their wives, whom they love, do they keep a tiny, small-scale version of their revels in a brothel. . . .

IRMA (*reprimanding her*): Carmen!

CARMEN: Excuse me, Madame . . . in a house of illusions. I was saying: do they keep their revels in a house of illusions tucked away in the back of their heads in miniature form, far off? But present?

IRMA: It's possible, child. No doubt they do. Like a Chinese lantern left over from a carnival, and waiting for the next one, or, if you prefer, like an imperceptible light in the imperceptible window of an imperceptible castle that they can enlarge instantly whenever they feel like going there to relax. (*Machine-gun fire.*) You hear that? They're approaching. They're out to get me.

CARMEN (*continuing her train of thought*): All the same, it must be nice in a real house.

IRMA (*more and more frightened*): They'll succeed in surrounding the house before George arrives. . . . One thing we mustn't forget—if ever we get out of this mess—is that the walls aren't sufficiently padded and the windows aren't well sealed. . . . One can hear all that's going on in the street. Which means that from the street one can hear what's going on in the house.

CARMEN (*still pensive*): In a real house, it must be nice. . . .

IRMA: Who knows! But Carmen, if my girls start bothering their heads about such things, it'll be the ruin of the brothel. I really think you miss your apparition. Look, I can do something for you. I did promise it to Regina, but I offer it to you. If you want to, of course. Someone rang me up yesterday and asked for a Saint Theresa. . . . (*A pause.*) Ah,

34

obviously, it's a come-down from the Immaculate
Conception to Saint Theresa, but it's not bad either. . . .
(*A pause.*) Well, what do you say? It's for a banker. Very
clean, you know. Not demanding. I offer it to you. If the
rebels are crushed, naturally.

CARMEN: I liked my dress and veil and rose-bush.

IRMA: There's a rose-bush in the "Saint Theresa" too. Think it
over.

(*A pause.*)

CARMEN: And what'll the authentic detail be?

IRMA: The ring. He's got it all worked out. The wedding ring.
You know that every nun wears a wedding ring, as a bride
of God. (CARMEN *makes a gesture of astonishment.*) That's
so. That's how he'll know he's dealing with a real nun.

CARMEN: What about the fake detail?

IRMA: It's almost always the same: black lace under the
homespun skirt. Well, how about it? You have the kind of
gentleness he likes. He'll be pleased.

CARMEN: It's really very kind of you, to think of him.

IRMA: I'm thinking of you.

CARMEN: You're so kind, Madame—I wasn't being ironic. The
thing to be said for your house is that it brings consolation.
You set up and prepare their secret theatres. . . . You've
got your feet on the ground. The proof is that you rake in
the money. Whereas they . . . their awakening must be
brutal. No sooner is it finished than it starts all over again.

IRMA: Luckily for me.

CARMEN: . . . starts all over again, and always the same
adventure. They'd like it never to end.

IRMA: You miss the entire point. When it's over, their minds are
clear. I can tell from their eyes. Suddenly they understand
mathematics. They love their children and their country.
Like you.

CARMEN (*puffing herself up*): I'm the daughter of a high-ranking
officer. . . .

IRMA: I know. There always has to be one in a brothel. But
bear in mind that General, Bishop and Judge are, in real
life. . . .

CARMEN: Which are you talking about?

IRMA: Real ones.

CARMEN: Which are real? The ones here?

IRMA: The others. In real life they're props of a display that they have to drag in the mud of the real and commonplace. Here, Comedy and Appearance remain pure, and the Revels intact.

CARMEN: The revels that I indulge in. . . .

IRMA (*interrupting her*): I know what they are: to forget theirs.

CARMEN: Do you blame me for that?

IRMA: And theirs are to forget yours. They, too, love their children. Afterwards.

(*Buzzing again, as before.* IRMA, *who has been sitting all the while near the apparatus, turns about, looks into the view-finder and puts the receiver to her ear. Carmen goes back to her accounts.*)

CARMEN (*without raising her head*): The Chief of Police?

IRMA (*describing the scene*): No. The waiter who just arrived. He's going to start complaining again . . . there he goes, he's flaring up because Elyane is handing him a white apron.

CARMEN: I warned you. He wants a pink one.

IRMA: Go to the Five-and-Ten tomorrow, if it's open. And buy a duster for the railwayman. A green one.

CARMEN: If only Elyane doesn't forget to drop the tip on the floor. He demands a true revolt. And dirty glasses.

IRMA: They all want everything to be as true as possible. . . . Minus something indefinable, so that it won't be true. (*Changing her tone.*) Carmen, it was I who decided to call my establishment a house of illusions, but I'm only the manager. Each individual, when he rings the bell and enters, brings his own scenario, perfectly thought out. My job is merely to rent the hall and furnish the props, actors and actresses. My dear, I've succeeded in lifting it from the ground—do you see what I mean? I unloosed it long ago and it's flying. I cut the moorings. It's flying. Or, if you like, it's sailing in the sky, and I with it. Well, my darling . . . may I say something tender—every madame

36

always, traditionally, has a slight partiality for one of her young ladies. . . .

CARMEN: I had noticed it, Madame, and I too, at times. . . .
(*She looks at Irma languidly.*)

IRMA (*standing up and looking at her*): I have a strange feeling, Carmen. (*A long pause.*) But let's continue. Darling, the house really does take off, leaves the earth, sails in the sky when, in the secrecy of my heart, I call myself, but with great precision, a keeper of a bawdy-house. Darling, when secretly, in silence, I repeat to myself silently, "You're a bawd, boss of a whore-house," darling, everything (*suddenly lyrical*), everything flies off—chandeliers, mirrors, carpets, pianos, caryatids and my studios, my famous studios: the studio known as the Hay Studio, hung with rustic scenes, the Studio of the Hangings, spattered with blood and tears, the Throne-room Studio, draped in velvet with a fleur-de-lis pattern, the Studio of Mirrors, the Studio of State, the Studio of Perfumed Foundations, the Urinal Studio, the Amphitrite Studio, the Moonlight Studio, everything flies off: studios—Oh! I was forgetting the studio of the beggars, of the tramps, where filth and poverty are magnified. To continue: studios, girls, . . . (*she thinks again.*) Oh! I was forgetting: the most beautiful of all, ultimate adornment, crown of the edifice—if the construction of it is ever completed. I speak of the Funeral Studio, adorned with marble urns, my Studio of Solemn Death, the Tomb! The Mausoleum Studio. . . . To continue: studios, girls, crystals, laces, balconies, everything takes it on the lam, rises up and carries me off!
(*A long pause. The two women are standing motionless, facing each other.*)

CARMEN: How well you speak.

IRMA (*modestly*): I went through elementary school.

CARMEN: So I assumed. My father, the artillery colonel. . . .

IRMA (*correcting her sharply*): You mean cavalry, my dear.

CARMEN: Excuse me. That's right. The cavalry colonel wanted me to have an education. Alas. . . . As for you, you've been successful. You've been able to surround your loveliness

37

with a sumptuous theatre, a gala, the splendours of which envelop you and hide you from the world. Your whoredom required such pomp. But what about me, am I to have only myself and be only myself? No, Madame. Thanks to vice and men's heartache, I too have had my moment of glory! With the receiver at your ear, you could see me through the view-finder, standing erect, sovereign and kind, maternal yet feminine, with my heel on the cardboard snake and the pink paper-roses. You could also see the bank-clerk from the National City kneeling before me and swooning when I appeared to him. Unfortunately he had his back to you and so you weren't aware of the ecstasy on his face and the wild pounding of my heart. My blue veil, my blue robe, my blue apron, my blue eyes. . . .

IRMA: They're hazel.

CARMEN: They were blue that day. For him I was Heaven in person descending on his brow. I was a Madonna to whom a Spaniard might have prayed and sworn an oath. He hymned me, fusing me with his beloved colour, and when he carried me to bed, it was into the blue that he penetrated. But I won't ever appear to him again.

IRMA: I've offered you Saint Theresa.

CARMEN: I'm not prepared, Mme Irma. One has to know what the client's going to require. Has everything been worked out?

IRMA: Every whore should be able—I hope you'll excuse me, but since we've gone so far, let's talk man to man—should be able to handle any situation.

CARMEN: I'm one of your whores, Mme Irma, and one of your best. I boast of it. In the course of an evening, I can . . .

IRMA: I'm aware of your feats. But when you start glorifying yourself as soon as you hear the word whore, which you keep repeating to yourself and which you flaunt as if it were a title, it's not quite the same as when I use the word to designate a function. But you're right, darling, to extol your profession and to glory in it. Make it shine. Let it illuminate you, if that's the only thing you have.

(*Tenderly*) I'll do all I can to help you. . . . You're not only

38

the purest jewel of all my girls, you're the one on whom I
bestow all my tenderness. But stay with me. . . . Would
you dare leave me when everything is cracking up
everywhere? Death—the real thing—is at my door, it's
beneath my windows. . . .
(*Machine-gun fire.*)
You hear?

CARMEN: The Army is fighting bravely.

IRMA: And the Rebels even more bravely. And we're in the
shadow of the cathedral, a few feet from the Archbishop's
Palace. There's no price on my head. No, that would be
too much to expect, but it's known that I serve supper to
prominent people. So they're out to get me. And there are
no men in the house.

CARMEN: There's Arthur.

IRMA: Are you trying to be funny? He's no man, he's my
stage-prop. Besides, as soon as his session is over, I'll send
him to look for George.

CARMEN: Assuming the worst. . . .

IRMA: If the rebels win? I'm a goner. They're workers. Without
imagination. Prudish and maybe chaste.

CARMEN: It won't take them long to get used to debauchery. Just
wait till they get a little bored. . . .

IRMA: You're wrong. Or else they won't let themselves get
bored. But I'm the one who's most exposed. For you it's
different. In every revolution there's the glorified whore who
sings an anthem and is virginified. That'll be you. The
others'll piously bring water for the dying to drink.
Afterwards . . . they'll marry you off. Would you like to
get married?

CARMEN: Orange blossoms, tulle . . .

IRMA: Wonderful! To you, getting married means masquerading.
Darling, you certainly are one of us. No, I can't imagine
you married either. Besides, what they're really dreaming of
doing is murdering us. We'll have a lovely death, Carmen.
It will be terrible and sumptuous. They may break into
my studios, shatter the crystals, tear the brocades and slit
our throats. . . .

CARMEN: They'll take pity. . . .

IRMA: They won't. They'll thrill at the thought that their fury is sacrilegious. All bedraggled, with caps on their heads, or in helmets and boots, they'll destroy us by fire and sword. It'll be very beautiful. We oughtn't to wish for any other kind of end, and you, you're thinking of leaving. . . .

CARMEN: But Mme Irma. . . .

IRMA: Yes, yes. When the house is about to go up in flames, when the rose is about to be stabbed, all you think of, Carmen, is fleeing.

CARMEN: If I wanted to be elsewhere, you know very well why.

IRMA: Your daughter is dead. . . .

CARMEN: Madame!

IRMA: Whether dead or alive, your daughter is dead. Think of the charming grave, adorned with daisies and artificial wreaths, at the far end of the garden . . . and that garden in your heart, where you'll be able to look after it. . . .

CARMEN: I'd have loved to see her again. . . .

IRMA: You'll keep her image in the image of the garden and the garden in your heart under the flaming robe of Saint Theresa. And you hesitate? I offer you the very finest of deaths, and you hesitate? Are you a coward?

CARMEN: You know very well I'm devoted to you.

IRMA: I'll teach you figures! The wonderful figures that we'll spend the nights together calligraphing.

CARMEN (*softly*): The war is raging. As you said, it's the horde.

IRMA (*triumphantly*): The horde, but we have our cohorts, our armies, our hosts, legions, battalions, vessels, heralds, clarions, trumpets, our colours, streamers, standards, banners . . . to lead us to catastrophe! Death? It's certain death, but with what speed and with what dash! . . . (*Melancholically*): Unless George is still all-powerful. . . . And above all if he can get through the horde and come and save us. (*A deep sigh.*): Now come and dress me. But first I want to see how Rachel's getting on.
(*Same business as before.* IRMA *glues her eye to the view-finder. A pause. She peers.*)
With this gadget I can see them and even hear their sighs.

40

(*A pause. She looks into the apparatus.*)
Christ is leaving with his paraphernalia. I've never been
able to understand why he has himself tied to the cross with
ropes he brings in a valise. Maybe they're ropes that have
been blessed. Where does he put them when he gets home?
Who the hell cares! Let's take a look at Rachel. (*She pushes
down another switch.*) Ah, they've finished. They're talking.
They're putting away the little arrows, the bow, the gauze
bandages, the white officer's cap. . . . No, I don't at all like
the way they're looking at each other: it's too candid and
straightforward. (*She turns to* CARMEN.) There you have the
dangers of regularity. It would be a catastrophe if my
clients and girls smiled at each other affectionately. It
would be an even greater catastrophe than if it were a
question of love. (*She presses the switch mechanically and
lays down the receiver. Pensively:*) Arthur's session must be
over. He'll be along in a minute. . . . Dress me.
CARMEN: What are you wearing?
IRMA: The cream-coloured négligé.
(CARMEN *opens the door of a closet and takes out the
négligé, while* IRMA *unhooks her suit.*)
Tell me, Carmen, what about Chantal? . . .
CARMEN: Madame?
IRMA: Yes. About Chantal, tell me, what do you know about
her?
CARMEN: I've questioned all the girls: Rosine, Elyane, Florence,
Marlyse. They've each prepared a little report. I'll let you
have them. But I didn't get much out of them. It's possible
to spy beforehand. During the fighting, it's harder. For one
thing, the camps are more sharply defined. You can choose.
When there's peace, it's too vague. You don't quite know
whom you're betraying. Nor even whether you're betraying.
There's no news about Chantal. They don't even know
whether she's still alive.
IRMA: But, tell me, you wouldn't have any scruples about it?
CARMEN: None at all. Entering a brothel means rejecting the
world. Here I am and here I stay. Your mirrors and
orders and the passions are my reality. What jewels are
41

you wearing?

IRMA : The diamonds. My jewels. They're the only things I have that are real. I feel everything else is sham. I have my jewels as others have little girls in gardens. Who's double-crossing? You're hesitating.

CARMEN : The girls all mistrust me. I collect their little report. I pass it on to you. You pass it on to the police. The police check on it. . . . Me, I know nothing.

IRMA : You're cautious. Give me a handkerchief.

CARMEN (*bringing a lace handkerchief*) : Viewed from here, where, in any case, men show their naked selves, life seems to me so remote, so profound, that it has all the unreality of a film or of the birth of Christ in the manger. When I'm in a room with a man and he forgets himself so far as to say to me: "The arsenal will be taken tomorrow night," I feel as if I were reading an obscene scrawl. His act becomes as mad, as . . . voluminous as those described in a certain way on certain walls. . . . No, I'm not cautious.

(*A knocking.* IRMA *gives a start. She rushes to the apparatus and, by means of a mechanism operated by a button, conceals it in the wall. In the course of the scene with Arthur, Carmen undresses and then dresses* IRMA, *so that the latter is ready just when the Chief of Police arrives.*)

IRMA : Come in!

(*The door opens. Enter* THE EXECUTIONER, *whom hereafter we shall call* ARTHUR. *Classical pimp's outfit: light grey suit, white felt hat, etc. He finishes knotting his tie.*)

IRMA (*examining him minutely*) : Is the session over? He went through it fast.

ARTHUR : Yes, the little geezer's buttoning up. He's pooped. Two sessions in half an hour. With all that shooting in the street, I wonder whether he'll get back to his hotel. (*He imitates the* JUDGE *in Scene Two.*) Minos judges you. . . . Minos weighs you . . . Cerberus? Bow-wow! Bow-wow! (*He shows his fangs and laughs.*) Hasn't the Chief of Police arrived?

IRMA : You went easy, I hope? Last time, the poor girl was laid up for two days.

42

(CARMEN *has brought the cream-coloured négligé.* IRMA *is now in her chemise.*)

ARTHUR: Don't pull that kind-hearted-whore stuff on me. Both last time and tonight she got what was coming to her: in dough and in wallops. Right on the line. The banker wants to see stripes on her back. So I stripe it.

IRMA: At least you don't get any pleasure out of it?

ARTHUR: Not with her. You're my only love. And a job's a job. I'm conscientious about my work.

IRMA (*sternly*): I'm not jealous of the girl, but I wouldn't want you to disable the personnel. It's getting harder and harder ro replace.

ARTHUR: I tried a couple of times to draw marks on her back with purple paint, but it didn't work. The old guy inspects her when he arrives and insists I deliver her in good shape.

IRMA: Paint? Who gave you permission? (*To* CARMEN) My Turkish slippers, darling.

ARTHUR (*shrugging his shoulders*): What's one illusion more or less! I thought I was doing the right thing. But don't worry. Now I whip, I flagellate, she screams, and he crawls.

IRMA: See to it she doesn't scream so loud. The house is being watched.

ARTHUR: The radio has just announced that all the north part of town was taken last night. And the Judge wants screaming. The Bishop's less dangerous. He's satisfied with pardoning sins.

CARMEN: Though he gets pleasure out of pardoning, he expects you to commit them. No, the best of the lot is the one you tie up, spank, whip and soothe, and then he snores.

ARTHUR: Who cuddles him? (*To Carmen*) You? Do you give him your breast?

CARMEN (*curtly*): I do my job right. And in any case, Mr. Arthur, you're wearing an outfit that doesn't allow you to joke. The pimp has a grin, never a smile.

IRMA: She's right.

ARTHUR: How much did you take in today?

IRMA (*on the defensive*): Carmen and I haven't finished the accounts.

ARTHUR: But I have. According to my calculations, it runs to a good two hundred.

IRMA: That's possible. In any case, don't worry. I don't cheat.

ARTHUR: I believe you, my love, but I can't help it: the figures arrange themselves in my head. Two hundred! War, rebellion, shooting, frost, hail, rain, showers of shit, nothing stops them! On the contrary. People are killing each other in the streets, the joint's being watched, but all the same, they come charging in. As for me, I've got you right at home, sweetie-pie, otherwise. . . .

IRMA (*bluntly*): You'd be cowering in a cellar, paralysed with fear.

ARTHUR (*ambiguously*): I'd do as the others do, my love. I'd wait to be saved by the Chief of Police. You're not forgetting my little percentage?

IRMA: I give you what you need.

ARTHUR: My love! I've ordered the silk shirts. And do you know what kind of silk? And what colour? In the purple silk of your blouse!

IRMA (*tenderly*): All right, cut it. Not in front of Carmen.

ARTHUR: Then it's O.K.?

IRMA (*weakening*): Yes.

ARTHUR: How much?

IRMA (*regaining her self-possession*): We'll see. I have to go over the accounts with Carmen. (*Winningly*) It'll be as much as I can. For the moment, you've absolutely got to go to meet George. . . .

ARTHUR (*with insolent irony*): I beg your pardon, my beloved?

IRMA (*curtly*): To go to meet Mr. George. To Police Headquarters if necessary, and to let him know that I'm relying only on him.

ARTHUR (*slightly uneasy*): You're kidding, I hope? . . .

IRMA (*with sudden sternness*): The tone of my last remark should answer your question. I'm no longer playing. Or, if you like not the same role. And there's no longer any need for you to play the mean, soft-hearted pimp. Do as I tell you, but first take the atomizer. (*To Carmen, who brings the object*) Give it to him. (*To Arthur*) And on your knees!

44

ARTHUR (*he puts one knee on the floor and sprays Irma*): In the
    street? All by myself? . . . Me? . . .
IRMA (*standing in front of him*): I've got to know what's
    happening to George. I can't remain unprotected.
ARTHUR: I'm here . . .
IRMA (*shrugging*): I've got to defend my jewels, my studios, my
    girls. The Chief of Police should have been here a half-
    hour ago. . . .
ARTHUR (*woefully*): Me in the street! . . . But it's hailing . . .
    they're shooting. . . . (*He points to his suit.*) And I got
    dressed up to stay here, to go walking through the corridors
    and look at myself in your mirrors. And also for you to see
    me dressed up as a pimp. . . . All I've got to protect me is
    the silk. . . .
IRMA (*to Carmen*): Let me have my bracelets, Carmen. (*To
    Arthur*) And you, spray.
ARTHUR: I'm not meant for outdoors. I've been living within
    your walls too long. Even my skin couldn't tolerate the
    fresh air . . . maybe if I had a veil. . . . What if I were
    recognized? . . .
IRMA (*irritated, and pivoting in front of the atomizer*): Hug the
    walls. (*A pause.*) Take this revolver.
ARTHUR (*frightened*): On me?
IRMA: In your pocket.
ARTHUR: My pocket! Imagine me having to shoot? . . .
IRMA (*gently*): So now you're crammed full of what you are?
    Gorged?
ARTHUR: Gorged, that's right. . . . (*A pause.*) Rested, gorged . . .
    but if I go out into the street. . . .
IRMA (*commandingly, but gently*): You're right. No revolver.
    But take off your hat and go where I tell you, and come
    back and let me know what's going on. You have a session
    this evening. Did you know? (*He tosses his hat away.*)
ARTHUR (*on his way to the door*): This evening? Another one?
    What is it?
IRMA: I thought I told you: a corpse.
ARTHUR (*with disgust*): What am I supposed to do with it?
IRMA: Nothing. You're to remain motionless, and you'll be

45

buried. You'll be able to rest.

ARTHUR: Ah, because I'm the one who. . . ? Ah, O.K. All right. Who's the client? Someone new?

IRMA (*mysteriously*): A very important person, and stop asking questions. Get going.

ARTHUR (*starting to leave, then hesitating, timidly*): Don't I get a kiss?

IRMA: When we come back. If we come back.

(*Exit* ARTHUR, *still on his knees.*)

(*But the door at the right has already opened and, without knocking,* THE CHIEF OF POLICE *enters. Heavy fur-lined coat, hat, cigar.* CARMEN *starts running to call Arthur back, but* THE CHIEF OF POLICE *steps in front of her.*)

THE CHIEF OF POLICE: No, no, stay, Carmen. I like having you around. As for the gigolo, let him find me.

(*He keeps his hat and coat on, does not remove his cigar from his mouth, but bows to* IRMA *and kisses her hand.*)

IRMA (*breathlessly*): Put your hand here. (*On her breast.*) I'm all tense. I'm still wrought up. I knew you were on your way, which meant you were in danger. I waited for you all a-tremble . . . while perfuming myself. . . .

THE CHIEF OF POLICE (*while taking off his hat, coat, gloves and jacket*): All right, that'll do. Let's cut the comedy. The situation's getting more and more serious—it's not desperate, but it will be before long—hap-pi-ly! The Royal Palace is surrounded. The Queen's in hiding. The city—it's a miracle that I got through—the city's being ravaged by fire and sword. Out there the rebellion is tragic and joyous, whereas in this house everything's dying a slow death. So, today's my day. By tonight I'll be in the grave or on a pedestal. So whether I love you or desire you is unimportant. How are things going at the moment?

IRMA: Marvellously. I had some great performances.

THE CHIEF OF POLICE (*impatiently*): What kind?

IRMA: Carmen has a talent for description. Ask her.

THE CHIEF OF POLICE (*to Carmen*): Tell me, Carmen, still. . . ?

CARMEN: Yes, sir, still. Still the pillars of the Empire: the Judge. . . .

46

THE CHIEF OF POLICE (*ironically*): Our allegories, our talking
weapons. And is there also. . . ?

CARMEN: As every week, a new theme.

(THE CHIEF OF POLICE *makes a gesture of curiosity*.)
This time it's the baby who gets slapped, spanked, tucked
in, then cries and is cuddled.

THE CHIEF OF POLICE (*impatiently*): Fine. But. . . .

CARMEN: He's charming, Sir. And so sad!

THE CHIEF OF POLICE (*irritably*): Is that all?

CARMEN: And so pretty when you unswaddle him. . . .

THE CHIEF OF POLICE (*with rising fury*): Are you pulling my leg,
Carmen? I'm asking you whether I'm in it?

CARMEN: Whether you're in it?

IRMA (*ironically, though we do not know with whom she is ironic*):
You're not in it.

THE CHIEF OF POLICE: Not yet? (*To Carmen.*) Well, yes or no, is
there a simulation. . . .

CARMEN (*bewildered*): Simulation?

THE CHIEF OF POLICE: You idiot! Yes! An impersonation of the
Chief of Police?

(*Very heavy silence.*)

IRMA: The time's not ripe. My dear, your function isn't noble
enough to offer dreamers an image that would console
them. Perhaps because it lacks illustrious ancestors? No, my
dear fellow. . . . You have to resign yourself to the fact that
your image does not yet conform to the liturgies of the
brothel.

THE CHIEF OF POLICE: Who's represented in them?

IRMA: You know who. You have your index-cards. (*She
enumerates on her fingers.*) There are two kings of France
with coronation ceremonies and different rituals, an admiral
at the stern of his sinking destroyer, a dey of Algiers
surrendering, a fireman putting out a fire, a goat attached
to a stake, a housewife returning from market, a
pickpocket, a robbed man who's bound and beaten up, a
Saint Sebastian, a farmer in his barn . . . but no chief of
police . . . nor colonial administrator, though there *is* a
missionary dying on the cross, and Christ in person.

47

THE CHIEF OF POLICE (*after a pause*): You're forgetting the mechanic.

IRMA: He doesn't come any more. What with tightening screws, he'd have ended by constructing a machine. And it might have worked. Back to the factory!

THE CHIEF OF POLICE: So not a single one of your clients has had the idea . . . the remotest idea, the barest suggestion. . . .

IRMA: No. I know you do what you can. You try hatred and love. But glory gives you the cold shoulder.

THE CHIEF OF POLICE (*forcefully*): My image is growing bigger and bigger. It's becoming colossal. Everything around me repeats and reflects it. And you've never seen it represented in this place?

IRMA: In any case, even if it were celebrated here, I wouldn't see anything. The ceremonies are secret.

THE CHIEF OF POLICE: You liar. You've got secret peep-holes in every wall. Every partition, every mirror, is rigged. In one place, you can hear the sighs, in another the echo of the moans. You don't need me to tell you that brothel tricks are mainly mirror tricks. . . . (*Very sadly*) Nobody yet! But I'll make my image detach itself from me. I'll make it penetrate into your studios, force its way in, reflect and multiply itself. Irma, my function weighs me down. Here, it will appear to me in the blazing light of pleasure and death. (*Musingly*) Of death.

IRMA: You must keep killing, my dear George.

THE CHIEF OF POLICE: I do what I can, I assure you. People fear me more and more.

IRMA: Not enough. You must plunge into darkness, into shit and blood. (*With sudden anguish*) And must kill whatever remains of our love.

THE CHIEF OF POLICE (*curtly*): Everything's dead.

IRMA: That's a fine victory. So you've got to kill what's around you.

THE CHIEF OF POLICE (*very irritated*): I repeat: I do what I can to prove to the nation that I'm a leader, a lawgiver, a builder. . . .

IRMA (*uneasily*): You're raving. Or else you really do expect to

48

build an empire. In which case you're raving.

THE CHIEF OF POLICE (*with conviction*): When the rebellion's been put down, and put down by me, when I've the nation behind me and been appealed to by the Queen, nothing can stop me. Then, and only then, will you see who I now am! (*Musingly*) Yes, my dear, I want to build an empire . . . so that the empire will, in exchange, build *me*. . . .

IRMA: . . . a tomb.

THE CHIEF OF POLICE (*somewhat taken aback*): But, after all, why not? Doesn't every conqueror have one? So? (*Exalted*) Alexandria! I'll have my tomb, Irma. And when the cornerstone is laid, you'll be my guest of honour.

IRMA: Thank you. (*To Carmen:*) Carmen, the tea.

THE CHIEF OF POLICE (*to Carmen, who is about to leave*): Just a minute, Carmen. What do you think of the idea?

CARMEN: That you want to merge your life with one long funeral, sir.

THE CHIEF OF POLICE (*aggressively*): Is life anything else? You seem to know everything—so tell me: in this sumptuous theatre where every moment a drama is performed—in the sense that the outside world says a mass is celebrated—what have you observed?

CARMEN (*after a hesitation*): As for anything serious, anything worth reporting, only one thing: that without the thighs it contained, a pair of pants on a chair is beautiful, sir. Emptied of our little old men, our ornaments are deathly sad. They're the ones that are placed on the catafalques of high dignitaries. They cover only corpses that never stop dying. And yet. . . .

IRMA (*to Carmen*): That's not what the Chief of Police is asking.

THE CHIEF OF POLICE: I'm used to Carmen's speeches. (*To Carmen:*) You were saying: and yet. . . ?

CARMEN: And yet, I'm sure that the sudden joy in their eyes when they see the cheap finery is really the gleam of innocence. . . .

THE CHIEF OF POLICE: People claim that our house sends them to Death. (*Suddenly a ringing.* IRMA *starts. A pause.*)

IRMA: Someone's opened the door. Who can it be at this hour? (*To Carmen*) Carmen, go down and shut the door. (CARMEN *exits. A rather long silence between* IRMA *and* THE CHIEF OF POLICE, *who remain alone.*)

THE CHIEF OF POLICE: My tomb!

IRMA: It was I who rang. I wanted to be alone with you for a moment. (*A pause, during which they look into each other's eyes seriously.*) Tell me, George. . . . (*She hesitates.*) Do you still insist on keeping up the game? No, no, don't be impatient. Aren't you tired of it?

THE CHIEF OF POLICE: But. . . . In a little while I'll be going home.

IRMA: If you can. If the rebellion leaves you free to go.

THE CHIEF OF POLICE: The rebellion is a game. From here you can't see anything of the outside, but every rebel is playing a game. And he loves his game.

IRMA: But supposing they let themselves be carried beyond the game? I mean if they get so involved in it that they destroy and replace everything. Yes, yes, I know, there's always the false detail that reminds them that at a certain moment, at a certain point in the drama, they have to stop, and even withdraw. . . . But what if they're so carried away by passion that they no longer recognize anything and leap, without realizing it, into. . . .

THE CHIEF OF POLICE: You mean into reality? What of it? Let them try. I do as they do, I penetrate right into the reality that the game offers us, and since I have the upper hand, it's I who score.

IRMA: They'll be stronger than you.

THE CHIEF OF POLICE: Why do you say "they'll be"? I've left the members of my bodyguard in one of your studios. So I'm always in contact with my various departments. All right, enough of that. Are you or aren't you the mistress of a house of illusions? Good. If I come to your place, it's to find satisfaction in your mirrors and their trickery. (*Tenderly*) Don't worry. Everything will be just as it's always been.

IRMA: I don't know why, but today I feel uneasy. Carmen

50

seems strange to me. The rebels——how shall I put it?—
have a kind of gravity. . . .

THE CHIEF OF POLICE: Their role requires it.

IRMA: No, no . . . of determination. They walk by the windows
threateningly, but they don't sing. The threat is in their
eyes.

THE CHIEF OF POLICE: What of it? Supposing it is, do you take
me for a coward? Do you think I should give up and go
home?

IRMA (*pensively*): No. Besides, I think it's too late.

THE CHIEF OF POLICE: Do you have any news?

IRMA: From Chantal, before she lit out. The power-house will
be occupied around 3 a.m.

THE CHIEF OF POLICE: Are you sure? Who told her?

IRMA: The partisans of the Fourth Sector.

THE CHIEF OF POLICE: That's plausible. How did she find out?

IRMA: It's through her that there were leaks, and through her
alone. So don't belittle my house. . . .

THE CHIEF OF POLICE: Your cat-house, my love.

IRMA: Cat-house, whore-house, bawdy-house. Brothel.
Fuckery. Call it anything you like. So Chantal's the only
one who's on the other side. . . . She lit out. But before
she did, she confided in Carmen, and Carmen's no fool.

THE CHIEF OF POLICE: Who tipped her off?

IRMA: Roger. The plumber. How do you imagine him? Young
and handsome? No. He's forty. Thick-set. Serious, with
ironic eyes. Chantal spoke to him. I put him out: too late.
He belongs to the Andromeda network.

THE CHIEF OF POLICE: Andromeda? Splendid. The rebellion's
riding high, it's moving out of this world. If it gives its sectors
the names of constellations, it'll evaporate in no time and
be metamorphosed into song. Let's hope the songs are
beautiful.

IRMA: And what if their songs give the rebels courage? What if
they're willing to die for them?

THE CHIEF OF POLICE: The beauty of their songs will make them
soft. Unfortunately, they haven't yet reached the point of
either beauty or softness. In any case, Chantal's tender

passions were providential.

IRMA: Don't bring God into. . . .

THE CHIEF OF POLICE: I'm a freemason. Therefore. . . .

IRMA: You? You never told me.

THE CHIEF OF POLICE (*solemnly*): Sublime Prince of the Royal Secret.

IRMA (*ironically*): You, a brother in a little apron! With a hood and taper and a little mallet! That's odd. (*A pause.*) You too?

THE CHIEF OF POLICE: Why? You too?

IRMA (*with mock solemnity*): I'm a guardian of far more solemn rites. (*Suddenly sad*) Since that's all I am now.

THE CHIEF OF POLICE: As usual, you're going to bring up our grand passion.

IRMA (*gently*): No, not our passion, but the time when we loved each other.

THE CHIEF OF POLICE: Well, would you like to give a historical account of it and deliver a eulogy? You think my visits would have less zest if you didn't flavour them with the memory of a pretended innocence?

IRMA: It's a question of tenderness. Neither the wildest concoctions of my clients nor my own fancies nor my constant endeavour to enrich my studios with new themes nor the passing of time nor the gilding and crystals nor bitter cold can dispel the moments when you cuddled in my arms or keep me from remembering them.

THE CHIEF OF POLICE: Do you really miss them?

IRMA (*tenderly*): I'd give my kingdom to relive a single one of them! And you know which one. I need just one word of truth—as when one looks at one's wrinkles at night, or rinses one's mouth. . . .

THE CHIEF OF POLICE: It's too late. (*A pause.*) Besides, we couldn't cuddle each other eternally. You don't know what I was already secretly moving towards when I was in your arms.

IRMA: I know that I loved you.

THE CHIEF OF POLICE: It's too late. Could you give up Arthur?

IRMA: It was you who forced him on me. You insisted on there

52

being a man here—against my better judgment—in
a domain that should have remained virgin. . . . You fool,
don't laugh. Virgin, that is, sterile. But you wanted a pillar,
a shaft, a phallus present—an upright bulk. Well, it's here.
You saddled me with that hunk of congested meat, that
milksop with wrestler's arms. He may look like a strong-
man at a fair, but you don't realize how fragile he is.
You stupidly forced him on me because you felt yourself
ageing.

THE CHIEF OF POLICE: Be still.

IRMA (*shrugging her shoulders*): And you relaxed here through
Arthur. I need him now. I have no illusions. I'm his man
and he relies on me, but I need that rugged shop-window
dummy hanging on to my skirts. He's my body, as it were,
but set beside me.

THE CHIEF OF POLICE (*ironically*): What if I were jealous?

IRMA: Of that big doll made up as an executioner in order to
satisfy a phony judge? You're kidding, but the spectacle of
me under the spectacle of that magnificent body never used
to bother you. . . . Let me repeat. . . .

THE CHIEF OF POLICE (*he slaps Irma, who falls on the sofa*): And
don't blubber or I'll break your jaw, and I'll send your
joint up in smoke. I'll set fire to your hair and bush and
I'll turn you loose. I'll light up the town with blazing
whores. (*Very gently*) Do you think I'm capable of it?

IRMA (*in a panting whisper*): Yes, darling.

THE CHIEF OF POLICE: All right, add up the accounts for me. If
you like, you can deduct Apollo's crêpe de Chine. And
hurry up. I've got to get back to my post. For the time
being, I have to act. Afterwards. . . . Afterwards, things'll
run themselves. My name will act in my place. Well, what
about Arthur?

IRMA (*submissively*): He'll be dead this evening.

THE CHIEF OF POLICE: Dead? You mean . . . really . . . really
dead?

IRMA (*with resignation*): Come, come, George, the way one dies
here.

THE CHIEF OF POLICE: Indeed? Meaning. . . .

53

IRMA: The Minister. . . . (*She is interrupted by the voice of* CARMEN.)

CARMEN (*in the wings*): Lock Studio 17! Elyane, hurry up! And lower the studio . . . no, no, wait. . . . (*We hear the sound of a rusty cog-wheel, the kind made by certain old lifts. Enter* CARMEN.) Madame, the Queen's Envoy is in the drawing-room. . . .

(*The door opens, left, and* ARTHUR *appears, trembling and with his clothes torn.*)

ARTHUR (*noticing the Chief of Police*): You here! You managed to get through?

IRMA (*rushing to his arms*): Darling! What's the matter? Are you hurt? Speak!

ARTHUR (*panting*): I tried to get to Police Headquarters. Impossible. The whole city's lit up with fires. The rebels are in control practically everywhere. I don't think you can get back, sir. I was able to reach the Royal Palace, and I saw the Grand Chamberlain. He said he'd try to come. I might add that he shook my hand. And then I left. The women are the most excited. They're urging the men to loot and kill. But what was most awful was a girl who was singing. . . .

(*A shot is heard. A window-pane is shivered. Also a mirror near the bed.* ARTHUR *falls down, hit in the forehead by a bullet coming from outside.* CARMEN *bends over him, then rises to her feet again. Then* IRMA *bends over him and strokes his forehead.*)

THE CHIEF OF POLICE: In short, I'm stuck in the whore-house. That means I'll have to act from the whore-house.

IRMA (*to herself, bent over Arthur*): Can it be that everything's slipping away? Slipping between my fingers? . . . (*bitterly*) I still have my jewels . . . my rocks . . . and perhaps not for long. . . .

CARMEN (*softly*): If the house is to be blown up. . . . Is Saint Theresa's costume in the closet, Mme Irma?

IRMA (*anxiously*): At the left. But first have Arthur removed. I'm going to receive the Envoy.

SCENE SIX

A public square, with patches of shadow. In the background, at some distance, we perceive the façade of the Grand Balcony, the blinds of which are drawn. CHANTAL *and* ROGER *are locked in embrace. Three men seem to be watching over them. Black suits. Black sweaters. They are holding machine-guns which are pointed at the Grand Balcony.*

CHANTAL: Keep me, if you will, my love, but keep me in your heart. And wait for me.

ROGER: I love you with your body, with your hair, your bosom, your belly, your guts, your fluids, your smells. Chantal, I love you in my bed. They. . . .

CHANTAL (*smiling*): They don't care a rap about me. But without them, *I'd* be nothing.

ROGER: You're mine. I . .

CHANTAL (*annoyed*): I know. You dragged me from the grave. And no sooner do I shake off my wrappings than, ungrateful wretch that I am, I gad about like a trollop. I plunge into the adventure, and I escape you. (*Suddenly with tender irony.*) But Roger, my love, you know I love you, you and only you.

ROGER: You've just said the word: you're escaping me. I can't follow you in your heroic and stupid course.

CHANTAL: Ah ha! You're jealous of whom, or what? People say that I soar above the insurrection, that I'm its soul and voice, and you—you're rooted to the ground. That's why you're sad. . . .

ROGER: Chantal, please, don't be vulgar. If you can help. . . .
(*One of the men draws near.*)

THE MAN (*to* ROGER): Well, is it yes or is it no?

ROGER: What if she stays there?

THE MAN: I'm asking you to let us have her for two hours.

ROGER: Chantal belongs. . . .

55

CHANTAL (*standing up*): To nobody!

ROGER: . . . To my section.

THE MAN: To the insurrection!

ROGER: If you want a woman to lead your men forward, then create one.

THE MAN: We looked for one, but there aren't any. We tried to build one up: nice voice, nice bosom, with the right kind of free and easy manner. But her eyes lacked fire, and you know that without fire. . . . We asked the North Section and the Port Section to let us have theirs; they weren't free.

CHANTAL: A woman like me? Another one? All I have is a hoarse voice and a face like an owl's. I give them or lend them for hatred's sake. I'm nothing, only my face, my voice, and inside me a sweet, poisonous kindness. D'you mean to tell me I have two popular rivals, two other poor devils? Let them come, I'll show them! I have no rival.

ROGER (*exploding*): I snatched her—snatched her from a grave. She's already escaping me and mounting to the sky. If I lend her to you. . . .

THE MAN: We're not asking you for that. If we take her, we're hiring her.

CHANTAL (*amused*): How much?

ROGER: Even if we let you have her to sing and spur on your district, if she gets bumped off we'll lose everything. No one can replace her.

THE MAN: She agreed to it.

ROGER: She doesn't belong to herself any more. She's ours. She's our sign. All that your women are good for is tearing up and carrying stones or reloading guns. I know that's useful, but. . . ·

THE MAN: How many women do you want in exchange?

ROGER (*thoughtfully*): Is a singer on the barricades as precious as all that?

THE MAN; How many? Ten women for Chantal?

(*A pause.*)

Twenty?

ROGER: Twenty women? You'd pay me twenty measly women, twenty oxen, twenty head of cattle? So Chantal's something

56

special? And do you know where she comes from?

CHANTAL (*to Roger, violently*): Every morning I go back—
because at night I'm ablaze—I go back to a hovel and sleep
—chastely, my love!—and drink myself into a stupor on
red wine. And I, with my grating voice, my sham anger, my
cameo eyes, my painted illumination, my Andalusian hair, I
comfort and enchant the rabble. They'll win and my victory
will be a strange one.

ROGER (*thoughtfully*): Twenty women for Chantal?

THE MAN (*sharply*): A hundred.

ROGER (*still pensively*): And it's probably because of her that
we'll win. She already embodies the Revolution. . . .

THE MAN: A hundred. You agree?

ROGER: Where are you taking her? And what'll she have to do?

CHANTAL: We'll see. Don't worry, I was born under a lucky
star. As for the rest of it, I realize my power. The people
love me, they listen to me, they follow me.

ROGER: What will she do?

THE MAN: Hardly anything. As you know, we're attacking the
Palace at dawn. Chantal will go in first. She'll sing from a
balcony. That's all.

ROGER: A hundred women. A thousand and maybe more. So
she's no longer a woman. The creature they make of her out
of rage and despair has her price. In order to fight against
an image Chantal has frozen into an image. The fight is no
longer taking place in reality, but in the lists. Field azure.
It's the combat of allegories. None of us know any longer
why we revolted. So she was bound to come round to that.

THE MAN: Well, is it yes? Answer, Chantal. It's for you to
answer.

CHANTAL (*to the Man*): I'd like us to be alone for a moment.
I've got something else to say.

(THE MAN *moves off and goes back into the shadow*.)

ROGER (*violently*): I didn't steal you for you to become a
unicorn or a two-headed eagle.

CHANTAL: You don't like unicorns.

ROGER: I've never been able to make love to them. (*He caresses
her*.) Nor to you either.

57

CHANTAL: You mean I don't know how to love. I disappoint you. Yet I love you. And you hired me out for a hundred female diggers.

ROGER: Forgive me. I need them. And yet I love you. I love you and I don't know how to tell you. I can't sing. And singing is the last resort.

CHANTAL: I'll have to leave before day-break. If the North Section has come through, the Queen will be dead in an hour. It'll be the end of the Chief of Police. If not, we'll never get out of this bedlam.

ROGER: One minute more, my love, my life. It's still night.

CHANTAL: It's the hour when night breaks away from the day, my dove, let me go.

ROGER: The minutes without you will be unbearable.

CHANTAL: We won't be separated, I swear to you. I'll speak to them in an icy tone and at the same time I'll murmur words of love for you. You'll hear them from here, and I'll hear yours.

ROGER: They may keep you, Chantal. They're strong—strong as death.

CHANTAL: Don't be afraid, my love. I know their power. Your sweetness and tenderness are stronger. I'll speak to them with severity. I'll tell them what the people demand. They'll listen to me because they'll be afraid. Let me go.

ROGER (screaming): Chantal, I love you!

CHANTAL: Ah, my love, it's because I love you that I must hurry.

ROGER: You love me?

CHANTAL: I love you because you're tender and sweet, you the hardest and sternest of men. And your sweetness and tenderness are such that they make you as light as a shred of tulle, subtle as a flake of mist, airy as a caprice. Your thick muscles, your arms, your thighs, your hands, are more unreal than the melting of day into night. You envelop me and I contain you.

ROGER: Chantal, I love you because you're hard and stern, you the tenderest and sweetest of women. And your sweetness and tenderness are such that they make you as stern as a

58

lesson, hard as hunger, inflexible as a block of ice. Your
breasts, your skin, your hair are more real than the
certainty of noon. You envelop me and I contain you.

CHANTAL: When I stand before them, when I speak to them, I'll
be hearing your sighs and moans and the beating of your
heart. Let me go.

(*He holds her back.*)

ROGER: You still have time. There's still some shadow along
the walls. You'll go round the back of the Archbishop's
Palace. You know the way.

ONE OF THE REBELS (*in a low voice*): It's time, Chantal. Day is
breaking.

CHANTAL: Do you hear? They're calling me.

ROGER (*suddenly irritated*): But why you? You'll never be able
to speak to them.

CHANTAL: I, better than anyone. I'm gifted.

ROGER: They're clever, cunning. . . .

CHANTAL: I'll invent gestures, postures, phrases. Before they
even say a word, I'll understand, and you'll be proud of my
victory.

ROGER: Let the others go. (*He cries out to the rebels.*) *You* go!
Or me, if you're afraid. I'll tell them they must give in,
because we're the law.

CHANTAL: Don't listen to him. He's drunk. (*To Roger*) All *they*
can do is fight, and all *you* can do is love me. That's the
role you've learned to play. As for me, it's something else.
At least the brothel has been of some use to me: it's taught
me the art of pretence, of acting. I've had to play so many
roles that I know almost all of them. And I've had so many
partners. . . .

ROGER: Chantal!

CHANTAL: And such artful ones, such cunning and eloquent
ones, that my skill and trickery and eloquence are
incomparable. I can be familiar with the Queen, the Hero,
the General, the heroic Troops . . . and can fool them all.

ROGER: You know all the roles, don't you? Just now, you were
reciting lines to me, weren't you?

CHANTAL: One learns fast. You yourself. . . .

59

(*The three rebels have drawn close.*)

ONE OF THE REBELS (*pulling* CHANTAL): Cut the speeches. Get going.

ROGER: Chantal, stay!

(CHANTAL *goes off, led by the rebels.*)

CHANTAL: I envelop you and I contain you, my love. . . .

(*She disappears in the direction of The Balcony, pushed by the three men.*)

ROGER (*alone*): . . . and I've had so many partners, and such artful ones, such cunning ones . . . that she did, after all, have to try to give them an answer. The one they wanted. In a little while she'll have cunning and artful partners. She'll be the answer they're waiting for.

(*As he speaks, the setting moves toward the left, the stage grows dark, and he himself, still speaking, moves off and into the wings. When the light goes on again, the setting of the next scene is in place.*)

SCENE SEVEN

The Funeral Studio in MME IRMA'S *listing of the Studios. The studio is in ruins. The lace and velvet are torn. The artificial wreaths are tattered. An impression of desolation.* IRMA'S *dress is in rags. So is the suit of* THE CHIEF OF POLICE. ARTHUR'S *corpse is lying on a kind of fake tomb of fake black marble. Nearby, a new character,* THE COURT ENVOY. *Embassy uniform. He is the only one unscathed.* CARMEN *is dressed as at the beginning. A tremendous explosion. Everything shatters.*

THE ENVOY (*in a tone both airy and grave*): For more centuries than I can tell, the centuries have worn themselves thin refining me . . . subtilizing me. . . . (*He smiles.*) From something or other about the explosion, from its power, in which was mingled a clinking of jewels and broken mirrors, I rather think it was the Royal Palace. (*The characters all look at each other, horror-stricken.*) Let us

not display any emotion. So long as we are not like that
.... (*He points to the corpse of Arthur.*)

IRMA: He didn't think he'd be acting his role of corpse this evening in earnest.

THE ENVOY (*smiling*): Our dear Minister of the Interior would have been delighted had not he himself met the same fate. It is unfortunately I who have had to replace him in his mission here, and I have no taste for pleasures of this kind. (*He touches Arthur's corpse with his foot.*) Yes, this body would have sent our dear Minister into raptures.

IRMA: Not at all, your Excellency. It's make-believe that these gentlemen want. The Minister desired a fake corpse. But this one is real. Look at it: it's truer than life. His entire being is speeding towards immobility.

THE ENVOY: He was therefore meant for grandeur.

THE CHIEF OF POLICE: Him? He was a spineless dummy.

THE ENVOY: He was, like us, haunted by a quest of immobility. By what we call the hieratic. And, in passing, allow me to pay tribute to the imagination responsible for there being a funeral parlour in this house.

IRMA (*proudly*): And you see only part of it.

THE ENVOY: Whose idea was it?

IRMA: The Wisdom of Nations, your Excellency.

THE ENVOY: It does things well. But we were talking about the Queen, to protect whom is my mission.

THE CHIEF OF POLICE: You're going about it in a curious way. The Palace, according to what you say. . . .

THE ENVOY (*smiling*): For the time being, Her Majesty is in safety. But time is pressing. The prelate is said to have been beheaded. The Archbishop's Palace has been ransacked. The Law Court and Military Headquarters have been routed. . . .

THE CHIEF OF POLICE: But what about the Queen?

THE ENVOY (*in a very light tone*): She's embroidering. For a moment she thought of nursing the wounded. But it was pointed out to her that, as the throne was threatened, she had to carry to an extreme the Royal prerogatives.

IRMA: Which are?

THE ENVOY : Absence. Her Majesty has retired to a chamber, in solitude. The disobedience of her people saddens her. She is embroidering a handkerchief. The design of it is as follows : the four corners will be adorned with poppy heads. In the middle of the handkerchief, embroidered in pale blue silk, will be a swan, resting on the water of a lake. That's the only point about which Her Majesty is troubled : will it be the water of a lake, a pond or a pool? Or simply of a tank or a cup? It is a grave problem. We have chosen it because it is insoluble, and the Queen can engross herself in an infinite meditation.

IRMA : Is the Queen amused?

THE ENVOY : Her Majesty is occupying herself in becoming entirely what she must be : the Queen. (*He looks at the corpse.*) She, too, is moving rapidly towards immobility.

IRMA : And she's embroidering.

THE ENVOY : No, Madame, I say the Queen is embroidering a handkerchief, for though it is my duty to describe her, it is also my duty to conceal her.

IRMA : Do you mean she's not embroidering?

THE ENVOY : I mean that the Queen is embroidering and that she is not embroidering. She picks her nose, examines the pickings and lies down again. Then, she dries the dishes.

IRMA : The Queen?

THE ENVOY : She is not nursing the wounded. She is embroidering an invisible handkerchief. . . .

THE CHIEF OF POLICE : By God! What have you done with Her Majesty? I want a straight answer. I'm not amused. . . .

THE ENVOY : She is in a chest. She is sleeping. Wrapped in the folds of Royalty, she is snoring. . . .

THE CHIEF OF POLICE (*threateningly*) : Is the Queen dead?

THE ENVOY (*unperturbed*) : She is snoring and she is not snoring. Her head, which is tiny, supports, without wavering, a crown of metal and stones.

THE CHIEF OF POLICE (*more and more threateningly*) : Enough of that. You said the Palace was in danger. . . . What's to be done? I still have almost the entire police force behind me. Those who are still with me are ready to die for me. . . .

They know who I am and what I'll do for them. . . . I, too, have my role to play. But if the Queen is dead, everything is jeopardized. *She's* my support, it's in her name that I'm working to make a name for myself. How far has the rebellion gone? I want a clear answer.

THE ENVOY: You can judge from the state of this house. And from your own. . . . All seems lost.

IRMA: You belong to the Court, your Excellency. Before coming here, I was with the troops. That's where I won my first spurs. I can assure you that I've known worse situations. The populace—from which I broke away with a kick of my heels—the populace is howling beneath my windows, which have been multiplied by the bombs: my house stands its ground. My rooms aren't intact, but they've held up. My whores, except for one lunatic, are on the job. If the centre of the Palace is a woman like me. . . .

THE ENVOY (*imperturbably*): The Queen is standing on one foot in the middle of an empty room, and she. . . .

THE CHIEF OF POLICE: That'll do! I've had enough of your riddles. For me, the Queen has to be someone. And the situation has to be concrete. Describe it to me exactly. I've no time to waste.

THE ENVOY: Whom do you want to save?

THE CHIEF OF POLICE: The Queen!

CARMEN: The flag!

IRMA: My hide!

THE ENVOY (*to the Chief of Police*): If you're eager to save the Queen—and, beyond her, our flag, and all its gold fringe, and its eagle, cords and pole, would you describe them to me?

THE CHIEF OF POLICE: Until now I've served the things you mention, and served them with distinction, and without bothering to know any more about them than what I saw. And I'll continue. What's happening about the rebellion?

THE ENVOY (*resignedly*): The garden gates will, for a moment longer, hold back the crowd. The guards are devoted, like us, with an obscure devotion. They'll die for their sovereign. They'll give their blood. Unhappily there won't be enough

of it to drown the rebellion. Sand bags have been piled up
in front of the doors. In order to confuse even reason, Her
Majesty removes herself from one secret chamber to
another, from the servants' hall to the Throne Room, from
the latrines to the chicken-coop, the chapel, the guard-
room. . . . She makes herself unfindable and thus attains
a threatened invisibility. So much for the inside of the
Palace.

THE CHIEF OF POLICE: What about the Generalissimo?

THE ENVOY: Gone mad. He wanders among the crowd, where
nobody will harm him, protected by his madness.

THE CHIEF OF POLICE: What about the Attorney-General?

THE ENVOY: Died of fright.

THE CHIEF OF POLICE: And the Bishop?

THE ENVOY: His case is more difficult. The Church is secretive.
Nothing is known about him. Nothing definite. His
decapitated head was said to have been seen on the
handlebars of a bicycle. Of course, the rumour was false.
We're therefore relying entirely on you. But your orders
aren't getting through.

THE CHIEF OF POLICE: Down below, in the corridors and studios,
I have enough loyal men to protect us all. They can remain
in contact with my offices. . . .

THE ENVOY (*interrupting him*): Are your men in uniform?

THE CHIEF OF POLICE: Of course. They're my bodyguard. Do
you imagine me with a bodyguard in sport jackets? They're
in uniform. Black ones. With my emblem. They're brave.
They, too, want to win.

THE ENVOY: To save what?

(*A pause.*)

Won't you answer? Would it perturb you to see things as
they are? To gaze at the world tranquilly and accept
responsibility for your gaze, whatever it might see?

THE CHIEF OF POLICE: But, after all, in coming to see me, you
did have something definite in mind, didn't you? You had a
plan? Let's hear it.

(*Suddenly a terrific blast. Both men, but not Irma, fall flat
on the floor, then stand up again and dust each other off.*)

64

THE ENVOY: That may have been the Royal Palace. Long live the
    Royal Palace!
IRMA: But then, just before . . . the explosion?
THE ENVOY: A royal palace is forever blowing up. In fact, that's
    exactly what it is: a continuous explosion.
    (*Enter* CARMEN. *She throws a black sheet over the corpse of
    Arthur and tidies things up a bit.*)
THE CHIEF OF POLICE (*aghast*): But the Queen. . . . Then the
    Queen's under the rubble?
THE ENVOY (*smiling mysteriously*): You need not worry. Her
    Majesty is in a safe place. And that phoenix, when dead,
    can rise up from the ashes of a royal palace. I can
    understand your impatience to prove your valour, your
    devotion . . . but the Queen will wait for you as long as
    necessary. (*To Irma:*) I must pay tribute, Madame, to your
    coolness. And to your courage. They are worthy of the
    highest respect. . . . (*Musingly*) of the highest. . . .
IRMA: You're forgetting to whom you're speaking. I may run a
    brothel, but I wasn't born of the marriage of the moon
    and a crocodile, I've lived among the people. . . . All the
    same, it was quite a blast. And the people. . . .
THE ENVOY (*severely*): That's behind you. When life departs, the
    hands cling to a sheet. What significance has that rag when
    you're about to penetrate into the providential fixity?
IRMA: Sir? Do you mean I'm at my last gasp?
THE ENVOY (*examining her, part by part*): Splendid head!
    Sturdy thighs! Solid shoulders!
IRMA (*laughing*): So I've been told, and it didn't make me lose
    my head. In short, I'll make a presentable corpse if the
    rebels act fast and if they leave me intact. But if the Queen
    is dead. . . .
THE ENVOY (*bowing*): Long live the Queen, Madame.
IRMA (*first taken aback, then irritated*): I don't like to be kidded!
    Pack up your nonsense, and clear out.
THE ENVOY (*spiritedly*): I've described the situation. The
    populace, in its joy and fury, is at the brink of ecstasy. It's
    for us to press it forward.
IRMA: Instead of standing here and talking drivel, go poke

C   65

around for the Queen in the rubble of the Palace and pull
her out. Even if slightly roasted. . . .

THE ENVOY (*severely*): No. A queen who's been cooked and
mashed up isn't presentable. And even when alive she was
less beautiful than you.

IRMA: Her lineage was more ancient . . . she was older. . . . And,
after all, maybe she was just as frightened as I.

THE CHIEF OF POLICE: It is in order to approach her, to be
worthy of her, that one makes such a mighty effort. But
what if one is Herself?

(CARMEN *stops in order to listen.*)

IRMA: I don't know how to talk. I'm always hemming and
hawing.

THE ENVOY: All must unfold in a silence that etiquette allows no
one to break.

THE CHIEF OF POLICE: I'm going to have the rubble of the Palace
cleared away. If, as you said, the Queen was in a chest, it
may be possible to save her.

THE ENVOY (*shrugging his shoulders*): It was made of rosewood!
And it was so old, so worn. . . . (*To Irma, running his hand
over the back of her neck*): Yes, it requires solid vertebrae
. . . they've got to carry several pounds   . .

THE CHIEF OF POLICE: . . . and resist the axe, don't they? Irma,
don't listen to him! (*To the Envoy.*) And what about me?
I'm the strong-man of this country, but it's because I've
based my power on the crown. I bamboozle the great
majority, but it's because I had the smart idea of serving
the Queen . . . even if at times I've seemed to do some
shabby things . . . seemed to, d'you hear? . . . It's not
Irma. . . .

IRMA (*to the Envoy*): I'm really very weak, your Excellency,
and very frail. Though a while ago I was boasting. . . .

THE ENVOY (*with authority*): Around this delicate and precious
kernel we'll forge a shell of gold and iron. But you must
make up your mind quickly.

THE CHIEF OF POLICE (*furiously*): Above me! So Irma would be
above *me*! All the trouble I've gone to in order to be
master would be wasted effort. Whereas, nice and snug in

66

her studio, all she'd have to do is nod her head. . . . If I'm
in power, I'm willing to impose Irma. . . .

THE ENVOY: Impossible. It's from her that you must derive
your authority. She must appear by divine right. Don't
forget that you're not yet represented in her studios.

IRMA: Allow me just a little more respite. . . .

THE ENVOY: A few seconds, for time is pressing.

THE CHIEF OF POLICE: If only there were some way of knowing
what the late sovereign would have thought of it. We can't
decide just like that. To appropriate a heritage. . . .

THE ENVOY (*scornfully*): You're knuckling under already. Do
you tremble if there's no authority above you to decide? But
it's for Mme Irma to declare. . . .

IRMA (*in a highfalutin tone*): In the records of our family, which
goes a long way back, there was some question of. . . .

THE ENVOY (*severely*): Nonsense, Mme Irma. In our vaults,
genealogists are working day and night. History is
submissive to them. I said we hadn't a minute to waste in
conquering our people, but beware! Although the populace
may worship you, its high-flown pride is capable of
sacrificing you. It sees you as red, either crimson or blood-
red. If it kills its idols and thrusts them into the sewers, it
will sweep you up with them. . . .

(*The same explosion is heard again.* THE ENVOY *smiles.*)

THE CHIEF OF POLICE: It's an enormous risk. . . .

CARMEN: That's for Mme Irma to decide. (*To Irma.*) The
ornaments are ready.

IRMA (*to the Envoy*): Are you quite sure of what you're saying?
Do you really know what's going on? What about your
spies?

THE ENVOY: They inform us as accurately as the peep-holes that
peer into your studios. (*Smiling.*) And I may add that we
consult them with the same pleasurable thrill. But we
must act fast. We're engaged in a race against the clock.
It's we or they. Mme. Irma, think speedily.

IRMA (*holding her head in her hands*): I'm hurrying, sir. I'm
approaching my destiny as fast as I can. (*To* CARMEN:) Go
see what they're doing.

CARMEN: I've locked them up.

IRMA: Get them ready.

THE ENVOY (*to Carmen*): What about you, what's to be done with you?

CARMEN: I'm here for eternity.

(*Exit* CARMEN.)

THE ENVOY: One other matter, a more delicate one. I mentioned an image that for some days now has been mounting in the sky of the revolution.

IRMA: The revolution has its sky too?

THE ENVOY: Don't envy it. Chantal's image is circulating in the streets. An image that resembles her and does not resemble her. She towers above the battles. At first, people were fighting against illustrious and illusory tyrants, then for freedom. Tomorrow they'll be ready to die for Chantal alone.

IRMA: The ungrateful wretch! She who was in such demand as Lucrezia Borgia.

THE CHIEF OF POLICE: She won't last. She's like me: she has neither father nor mother. And if she becomes an image, we'll make use of it. (*A pause.*) . . . A mask. . . .

THE ENVOY: Everything beautiful on earth you owe to masks. (*Suddenly a bell rings.* IRMA *is about to dart forward, but stops.*)

IRMA (*to the Chief of Police*): It's Carmen. What's she saying? What are they doing?

(THE CHIEF OF POLICE *lifts one of the earphones.*)

THE CHIEF OF POLICE (*transmitting the message*): While waiting to go home, they're standing around looking at themselves in the mirrors.

IRMA: Tell her to smash the mirrors or veil them.

(*A silence. Then a burst of machine-gun fire.*)

My mind's made up. I presume I've been summoned from all eternity and that God will bless me. I'm going to prepare myself by prayer.

THE ENVOY (*gravely*): Do you have the outfits?

IRMA: My closets are as famous as my studios. (*Suddenly worried.*) But everything must be in an awful state! The

68

bombs, the plaster, the dust. Tell Carmen to brush the costumes! (*To the Chief of Police*:) George . . . this is our last minute together! From now on, we'll no longer be us. . . .

(THE ENVOY *discreetly moves off and goes to the window.*)

THE CHIEF OF POLICE (*tenderly*): But I love you.

THE ENVOY (*turning around, and in a tone of detachment*): Think of that mountain north of the city. All the labourers were at work when the rebellion broke out. . . . (*A pause.*) I refer to a project for a tomb. . . .

THE CHIEF OF POLICE (*greedily*): What's the plan of it?

THE ENVOY: Later. A mountain of red marble hollowed out with rooms and niches, and in the middle a tiny diamond sentry-box.

THE CHIEF OF POLICE: Will I be able to stand there—or sit—and keep vigil over my entire death?

THE ENVOY: He who gets it will be there—dead—for eternity. The world will centre about it. About it will rotate the planets and the suns. From a secret point of the same room will run a road that will lead, after many and many a complication, to another room where mirrors will reflect to infinity . . . I say infinity. . . .

THE CHIEF OF POLICE: O.K.!

THE ENVOY: . . . . the image of a dead man.

IRMA (*hugging the Chief of Police to her*): So I'll be real? My robe will be real? My lace, my jewels will be real? The rest of the world. . . .

(*Machine-gun fire.*)

THE ENVOY (*after a last glance through the shutters*): Yes, but make haste. Go to your apartments. Embroider an interminable handkerchief. . . . (*To the Chief of Police*:) You, give your last orders to your last men. (*He goes to a mirror, takes from his pocket a whole collection of decorations and fastens them to his tunic.*) (*In a vulgar tone*) And make it snappy. I don't have time to listen to your crap.

SCENE EIGHT

The scene is the balcony itself, which projects beyond the façade of the brothel. The shutters, which face the audience, are closed. Suddenly, all the shutters open by themselves. The edge of the balcony is at the very edge of the footlights. Through the windows can be seen THE BISHOP, THE GENERAL *and* THE JUDGE, *who are getting ready. Finally, the French windows are flung wide open. The three men come out on the balcony. First* THE BISHOP, *then* THE GENERAL, *then* THE JUDGE. *They are followed by the Hero. Then comes* THE QUEEN: MME IRMA, *wearing a diadem on her brow and an ermine cloak. All the characters step forward and take their positions with great timidity. They are silent. They simply show themselves. All are of huge proportions, gigantic—except the Hero, that is,* THE CHIEF OF POLICE—*and are wearing their ceremonial garments, which are torn and dusty. Then, near them, but not on the balcony, appears the beggar. In a gentle voice, he cries out:*

THE BEGGAR: Long live the Queen! (*He goes off timidly, as he came.*)
(*Finally, a strong wind stirs the curtains:* CHANTAL *appears.* THE QUEEN *bows to her. A shot.* CHANTAL *falls.* THE GENERAL *and* THE QUEEN *carry her away dead.*)

SCENE NINE

IRMA'S *room, which looks as if it had been hit by a hurricane. Rear, a large two-panelled mirror which forms the wall. Right, a door; left, another. Three cameras on tripods. Next to each of them is a photographer, three very wide-awake young men with ironic expressions. Each is wearing a black leather jacket and close-fitting blue jeans. Enter, in turn, very timidly, right,* THE BISHOP *and, left,* THE JUDGE *and* THE GENERAL. *On seeing each other, they bow deeply. Then,* THE GENERAL *salutes and* THE BISHOP *blesses* THE GENERAL.

THE JUDGE (*with a sigh of relief*): What we've been through!

THE GENERAL: And it's not over! We have to invent an entire life. . . . That's hard. . . .

THE BISHOP: Hard or not, we've got to go through with it. We can no longer back out. Before entering the carriage. . . .

THE GENERAL: The slowness of the carriage!

THE BISHOP: . . . entering the carriage, it was still possible to chuck the whole business. But now. . . .

THE JUDGE: Do you think we were recognized? I was in the middle, hidden by your profiles. Opposite me, Irma. . . . (*The name astonishes him.*) Irma? The Queen. . . . The Queen hid my face. . . . Do you think we were?

THE BISHOP: No danger of that. You know whom I saw . . . at the right (*unable to keep from laughing*) with his fat, good-natured mug and pink cheeks, though the town was in smithereens? (*The other two smile.*) With his dimples and decayed teeth? And who threw himself on my hand . . . I thought to bite me, and I was about to pull away my fingers . . . to kiss my ring? Who? My fruit-and-vegetable man. (THE JUDGE *laughs.*)

THE GENERAL (grimly): The slowness of the carriage. The carriage wheels on the people's feet and hands! The dust!

THE JUDGE (*uneasily*): I was opposite the Queen. Through the back window, a woman. . . .

THE BISHOP (*continuing his account*): I saw her too, at the left-hand door, she was running along and throwing kisses at us!

THE GENERAL (*more and more grimly*): The slowness of the carriage! We moved forward so slowly amidst the sweaty mob! Their roars were like threats, but they were only cheering. Someone could have hamstrung the horses, fired a shot, could have unhitched the traces and harnessed *us*, attached us to the shaft or the horses, could have drawn and quartered us or turned us into draught-horses. But no. Just flowers tossed from a window, and a people hailing its queen, who stood upright beneath her golden crown. (*A pause.*) And the horses going at a walking pace . . . and the Envoy standing on the footboard!

71

(*A silence.*)

THE BISHOP (*ironically*): No one could have recognized us. We were in the gold and glitter. They were blinded. It hit them in the eye. . . .

THE JUDGE: It wouldn't have taken much. . . .

THE BISHOP (*same*): Exhausted by the fighting, choked by the dust, the people stood waiting for the procession. The procession was all they saw. In any case, we can no longer back out. We've been chosen.

THE GENERAL: By whom?

THE BISHOP (*with sudden grandiloquence*): By glory in person.

THE GENERAL: This masquerade?

THE BISHOP: It lies with us for this masquerade to change meaning. First, we must use words that magnify. We must act fast, and with precision. No errors allowed. (*With authority*) As for me, instead of being merely the symbolic head of the country's church, I've decided to become its actual head. Instead of blessing and blessing and blessing until I've had my fill, I'm going to sign decrees and appoint priests. The clergy is being organized. A basilica is under construction. It's all in there. (*He points to a folder under his arm.*) Full of plans and projects. (*To the Judge*) What about you?

THE JUDGE (*looking at his wristwatch*): I have an appointment with a number of magistrates. We're drafting bills, we're revising the legal code. (*To the General*) What about you?

THE GENERAL: Oh, me, your ideas drift through my poor head like smoke through a log shanty. The art of war's not something you can master just like that. The general-staffs. . . .

THE BISHOP (*interrupting*): Like everything else, the fate of arms can be read in your stars. Read your stars, damn it!

THE GENERAL: That's easy to say. But when the Hero comes back, planted firmly on his rump, as if on a horse. . . . For, of course, nothing's happened yet?

THE BISHOP: Nothing. But let's not crow too soon. Though his image hasn't yet been consecrated by the brothel, it still may. If so, we're done for. Unless you make a positive effort to seize power.

(*Suddenly, he breaks off. One of the photographers has
cleared his throat, as if to spit. Another has snapped his
fingers like a Spanish dancer.*)

THE BISHOP (*severely*): Indeed, you're here. Please do your job
quickly, and in silence, if possible. You're to take each of
our profiles, one smiling, the other rather stern.

FIRST PHOTOGRAPHER: We'll do our job, don't worry. (*To the
Bishop:*) Get set for prayer, because the world ought to be
bombarded with the picture of a pious man.

THE BISHOP (*without moving*): In fervent meditation.

FIRST PHOTOGRAPHER: Right, fervent. Get set.

THE BISHOP (*ill at ease*): But . . . how?

FIRST PHOTOGRAPHER: Don't you know how to compose yourself for prayer? Okay, facing both God and the camera.
Hands together. Head up. Eyes down. That's the classical
pose. A return to order, a return to classicism.

THE BISHOP (*kneeling*): Like this?

FIRST PHOTOGRAPHER (*looking at him with curiosity*): That's
it. . . . (*He looks at the camera.*) No you're not in the
frame. . . . (*Shuffling on his knees, the* BISHOP *places himself
in front of the camera.*) Okay.

SECOND PHOTOGRAPHER (*to the Judge*): Would you mind pulling
a longer face? You don't quite look like a judge. A little
longer.

THE JUDGE: Horselike? Sullen?

SECOND PHOTOGRAPHER: Horselike and sullen, my Lord. And
both hands in front, on your brief. What I want is a shot of
the Judge. A good photographer is one who gives a
definitive image. Perfect.

FIRST PHOTOGRAPHER (*to the Bishop*): Turn your head . . . just
a little. . . . (*He turns the Bishop's head.*)

THE BISHOP (*angrily*): You're unscrewing the neck of a prelate!

FIRST PHOTOGRAPHER: I want a three-quarter view of you
praying, my Lord.

SECOND PHOTOGRAPHER (*to the Judge*): My Lord, if you possibly
can, a little more severity . . . with a pendulous lip.
(*Crying out*) That's it! Perfect! Stay that way! (*He rushes*

73

behind his camera, but there is a flash before he gets there.
THE FIRST PHOTOGRAPHER *has just taken his shot.* THE
SECOND PHOTOGRAPHER *puts his head under the black hood
of his camera.*)

THE GENERAL (*to the Third Photographer*): The finest pose is
Poniatovsky's.

THIRD PHOTOGRAPHER (*striking a pose*): With the sword?

THE GENERAL: No, no. That's Lafayette. No, with the arm
extended and the marshal's baton. . . .

THIRD PHOTOGRAPHER: Ah, you mean Wellington?

THE GENERAL: Unfortunately, I don't have a baton. . . .
(*Meanwhile, the* FIRST PHOTOGRAPHER *has gone back to the
Bishop, who has not moved, and looks him over silently.*)

THIRD PHOTOGRAPHER (*to the General*): We've got just what we
need. Here, now strike the pose. (*Rolls up a sheet of paper
in the form of a marshal's baton. He hands it to the General,
who strikes a pose, and then dashes to his camera. A flash:
the* SECOND PHOTOGRAPHER *has just taken his shot.*)

THE BISHOP (*to the First Photographer*): I hope the negative
comes out well. Now we'll have to flood the world with a
picture of me receiving the Eucharist. Unfortunately, we
don't have a Host on hand. . . .

FIRST PHOTOGRAPHER: Leave it to us, Monsignor. Newspapermen
are a resourceful bunch. (*Calls out*) My Lord!
(THE JUDGE *approaches.*)
I'm going to try a stunt. Lend me a hand a minute. (*Without
further ado, he takes him by the hand and sets him in place.*)
But I want only your hand to show . . . there . . . roll up
your sleeve a little . . . above Monsignor's tongue. More.
Okay. (*Still fumbling in his pocket. To the Bishop*) Stick out
your tongue. More. Okay. (*Still fumbling in his pocket. A
flash:* THE GENERAL *has just been photographed; he resumes
his natural pose.*) Damn it! I don't have a thing! (*He looks
about. To the General*) That's perfect. May I? (*Without
waiting for an answer, he takes the General's monocle from
his eye and goes back to the group formed by* THE BISHOP
and THE JUDGE. *He makes* THE JUDGE *hold the monocle
above the Bishop's tongue as if it were a Host, and he*

74

rushes to his camera. A flash.)

(THE QUEEN, *who has entered with* THE ENVOY, *has been watching these proceedings for some moments.*)

THE ENVOY: It's a true image, born of a false spectacle.

FIRST PHOTOGRAPHER (*cynically*): That's common practice, your Majesty. When some rebels were captured, we paid a militiaman to bump off a chap I'd just sent to buy me a packet of cigarettes. The photo shows a rebel shot down while trying to escape.

THE QUEEN: Monstrous!

THE ENVOY: But have things ever happened otherwise? History was lived so that a glorious page might be written, and then read. It's reading that conuts. (*To the photographers*) Gentlemen, the Queen informs me that she congratulates you. She asks that you return to your posts.

(*The* THREE PHOTOGRAPHERS *put their heads under the black hoods of their cameras.*)

(*A silence.*)

THE QUEEN (*in a low voice, as if to herself*): Isn't he here?

THE ENVOY (*to the Three Figures*): The Queen would like to know what you're doing, what you plan to do.

THE BISHOP: We've been recovering as many dead bodies as possible. We were planning to embalm them and lodge them in our heaven. Your grandeur requires your having slaughtered the rebels wholesale. We shall keep for ourselves only a few of our fallen martyrs, to whom we shall pay honour that will honour us.

THE QUEEN (*to the Envoy*): That will serve my glory, will it not?

THE ENVOY (*smiling*): The massacres, too, are revels wherein the people indulge to their heart's content in the pleasure of hating us. I am speaking, to be sure, of "our" people. They can at last set up a statue to us in their hearts so as to shower it with blows. At least, I hope so.

THE QUEEN: Does that mean that leniency and kindness are of no avail?

THE ENVOY (*smiling*): A St. Vincent de Paul Studio?

THE QUEEN (*testily to the Judge*): You, my Lord, what's being done? I'd ordered fewer death penalties and more

75

sentences to forced labour. I hope the underground galleries are finished? (*To the Envoy*) It's the word galley-slaves that made me think of the galleries of the Mausoleum. Are they finished?

THE JUDGE: Completely. And open to the public on Sundays. Some of the arches are completely adorned with the skeletons of prisoners who died during the digging.

THE QUEEN (*in the direction of the Bishop*): Very good. What about the Church? I suppose that anyone who hasn't done at least a week's work on this extraordinary chapel is in a state of mortal sin?

(THE BISHOP *bows. To the General*) As for you, I'm aware of your severity. Your soldiers are watching over the workers, and they thoroughly deserve the fine name of builders. (*Smiling gently, with feigned fatigue.*) For, as you know, gentlemen, I plan to present this tomb to the Hero. You know how downcast he feels, don't you, and how he suffers at not yet having been impersonated?

THE GENERAL (*plucking up courage*): He'll have a hard time attaining glory. The places have been filled for ages. Every niche has its statue. (*Fatuously:*) We, at least. . . .

THE JUDGE: That's how it always is when one wants to start from the bottom. And particularly by rejecting or neglecting the traditional. The established order of things, as it were.

THE QUEEN (*suddenly vibrant*): Yet it was he who saved everything. He wants glory. He insists on breaking open the gates of legend, but he has allowed you to carry on with your ceremonies.

THE BISHOP (*arrogantly*): To be frank, Madame, we're no longer concerned with that. As for me, my skirt hampers me, and my hands get caught in the lace. We're going to have to act.

THE QUEEN (*indignantly*): Act? You? You mean to say you're going to strip us of our power?

THE JUDGE: We have to fulfil our functions, don't we?

THE QUEEN: Functions! You're planning to overthrow him, to lower him, to take his place!

THE BISHOP: Somewhere in time—in time or in space!—perhaps

76

there exist high dignitaries invested with absolute dignity and attired with veritable ornaments. . . .

THE QUEEN (*very angrily*): Veritable! And what about those? You mean that those you're wrapped and swathed in—my whole paraphernalia!—which come from my closets, aren't veritable?

THE BISHOP (*pointing to the Judge's ermine, the silk of his robe, etc.*): Rabbit, sateen, machine-made lace . . . you think we're going to be satisfied with make-believe to the end of our days?

THE QUEEN (*outraged*): But this morning. . . .
(*She breaks off. Enter* THE CHIEF OF POLICE, *quietly, humbly.*)
George, beware of them.

THE CHIEF OF POLICE (*trying to smile*): I think that . . . victory . . . we've won the day. May I sit down?
(*He sits down. Then he looks about, as if questioning everyone.*)

THE ENVOY (*ironically*): No, nobody's come yet. Nobody has yet felt the need to abolish himself in your fascinating image.

THE CHIEF OF POLICE: That means the projects you submitted to me aren't very effective. (*To the Queen*) Nothing? Nobody?

THE QUEEN (*very gently*): Nobody. And yet, the blinds have been drawn again. The men ought to be coming in. Besides, the apparatus has been set up; so we'll be informed by a full peal of bells.

THE ENVOY (*to the Chief of Police*): You didn't care for the project I submitted to you this morning. Yet that's the image that haunts you and that ought to haunt others.

THE CHIEF OF POLICE: Ineffectual.

THE ENVOY (*showing a photographic negative*): The executioner's red coat and his axe. I suggested amaranth red and the steel axe.

THE QUEEN (*testily*): Studio 14, known as the Studio of Executions. Already been done.

THE JUDGE (*making himself agreeable, to the Chief of Police*) Yet you're feared.

THE CHIEF OF POLICE: I'm afraid that they fear and envy a man,

77

but ... (*groping for words*) ... but not a wrinkle, for example, or a curl ... or a cigar ... or a whip. The latest image that was proposed to me. .... I hardly dare mention it to you.

THE JUDGE: Was it ... very audacious?

THE CHIEF OF POLICE: Very. Too audacious. I'd never dare tell you what it was. (*Suddenly, he seems to make up his mind.*) Gentlemen, I have sufficient confidence in your judgment and devotion. After all, I want to carry on the fight by boldness of ideas as well. It was this: I've been advised to appear in the form of a gigantic phallus, a prick of great stature. ....

(*The Three Figures and the Queen are dumbfounded.*)

THE QUEEN: George! You?

THE CHIEF OF POLICE: What do you expect? If I'm to symbolize the nation, your joint. ....

THE ENVOY (*to the Queen*): Allow him, Madame. It's the tone of the age.

THE JUDGE: A phallus? Of great stature? You mean—enormous?

THE CHIEF OF POLICE: Of my stature.

THE JUDGE: But that'll be very difficult to bring off.

THE ENVOY: Not so very. What with new techniques and our rubber industry, remarkable things can be worked out. No I'm not worried about that, but rather ... (*turning to the Bishop*) ... what the Church will think of it?

THE BISHOP (*after reflection, shrugging his shoulders*): No definite pronouncement can be made this evening. To be sure, the idea is a bold one. (*To the Chief of Police*) But if your case is desperate, we shall have to examine the matter. For ... it would be a formidable figure-head, and if you were to transmit yourself in that guise to posterity. ....

THE CHIEF OF POLICE (*gently*): Would you like to see the model?

THE JUDGE (*to the Chief of Police*): It's wrong of you to be impatient. *We* waited two thousand years to perfect our roles. Keep hoping. ....

THE GENERAL (*interrupting him*): Glory is achieved in combat. You haven't enough illustrious Waterloos to your credit.

Keep fighting, or sit down and wait out the regulation two thousand years.

(*Everyone laughs.*)

THE QUEEN (*violently*): You don't care a damn about his suffering. And it was I who singled you out! I who fished you out of the rooms of my brothel and hired you for his glory. And you agreed to serve him.

(*A pause.*)

THE BISHOP (*firmly*): It is at this point that a question, and a very serious one, arises: are you going to use what we represent, or are we (*he points to the other two Figures*) going to use you to serve what we represent?

THE QUEEN (*flaring up*): Your conditions, you? Puppets who without their rabbit, as you put it, would be nothing, you, a man who was made to dance naked—in other words, skinned!—on the public squares of Seville and Toledo! and who danced! To the click of castanets! Your conditions, my Lord?

THE BISHOP: That day I *had* to dance. As for the rabbit, it's what it *must* be—the sacred image of ermine—it has the same power.

THE CHIEF OF POLICE: For the time being, but. . . .

THE BISHOP (*getting excited*): Exactly. So long as we were in a room in a brothel, we belonged to our own fantasies. But once having exposed them, having named them, having proclaimed them, we're now tied up with human beings, tied to you, and forced to go on with this adventure according to the laws of visibility.

THE CHIEF OF POLICE: You have no power. I alone. . . .

THE BISHOP: Then we shall go back to our rooms and there continue the quest of an absolute dignity. We ought never to have left them. For we were content there, and it was you who came and dragged us away. For ours was a happy state. And absolutely safe. In peace, in comfort, behind shutters, behind padded curtains, protected by a police force that protects brothels, we were able to be a general, judge and bishop to the point of perfection and to the point of rapture! You tore us brutally from that delicious,

79

untroubled state.

THE GENERAL (*interrupting the Bishop*): My breeches! What joy
when I pulled on my breeches! I now sleep in my general's
breeches. I eat in my breeches, I waltz—*when* I waltz—in
my breeches, I live in my general's breeches. I'm a general
the way one is a priest.

THE JUDGE: I'm just a dignity represented by a skirt.

THE GENERAL (*to the Bishop*): At no moment can I prepare
myself—I used to start a month in advance!—prepare
myself for pulling on my general's boots and breeches. I'm
rigged in them for all eternity. By Jove, I no longer dream.

THE BISHOP (*to the Chief of Police*): You see, he no longer
dreams. Our ornamental purity, our luxurious and barren
—and sublime—appearance has been eaten away. It's gone
forever. Well and good. But the taste of that bitter delight
of responsibility of which I've spoken has remained with us,
and we find it to our liking. Our rooms are no longer
secret. You hurt us by dragging us into the light. But
as for dancing? You spoke of dancing? You referred to
that notorious afternoon when, stripped—or skinned,
whichever word amuses you—stripped of our priestly
ornaments, we had to dance naked on the cathedral square.
I danced, I admit it, with people laughing at me, but at
least I danced. Whereas now, if ever I have an itch for that
kind of thing, I'll have to go on the sly to the Balcony,
where there probably is a room prepared for prelates who
like to be ballerinas a few hours a week. No, no. . . .
We're going to live in the light, but with all that that
implies. We—magistrate, soldier, prelate—we're going to
act in such a way as to impoverish our ornaments
unceasingly! We're going to render them useful! But in
order that they be of use, and of use to us—since it's your
order that we've chosen to defend—you must be the first
to recognize them and pay homage to them.

THE CHIEF OF POLICE (*calmly*): I shall be not the hundred-
thousandth-reflection-within-a-reflection in a mirror, but
the One and Only, into whom a hundred thousand want to
merge. If not for me, you'd have all been done for. The

expression "beaten hollow" would have had meaning. (*He is going to regain his authority increasingly.*)

THE QUEEN (*to the Bishop, insinuatingly*): You happen to be wearing that robe this evening simply because you were unable to clear out of the studios in time. You just couldn't tear yourself away from one of your hundred thousand reflections, but the clients are beginning to come back. . . . There's no rush yet, but Carmen has recorded several entries. . . . (*To the Chief of Police*) Don't let them intimidate you. Before the revolt, there were lots of them. . . . (*To the Bishop*) If you hadn't had the abominable idea of having Chantal assassinated. . . .

THE BISHOP (*frightened*): A stray bullet!

THE QUEEN: Stray or not, Chantal was assassinated on *my* balcony! When she came back here to see me, to visit her boss. . . .

THE BISHOP: I had the presence of mind to make her one of our saints.

THE CHIEF OF POLICE: A traditional attitude. A churchman's reflex. But there's no need to congratulate yourself. The image of her on our flag has hardly any power. Or rather. . . . I've had reports from all quarters that owing to the possibility that she was playing a double game, Chantal has been condemned by those she was supposed to save. . . .

THE QUEEN (*anxiously*): But then the whole business is starting all over again?

(*From this point on* THE QUEEN *and* THE CHIEF OF POLICE *will seem very agitated.* THE QUEEN *will go to a window and draw the curtains after trying to look out into the street.*)

THE ENVOY: All of it.

THE GENERAL: Are we going to have to . . . to get into the carriage again? The slowness of the carriage!

THE BISHOP: If I had Chantal shot, and then canonized, if I had her image blazoned on our flag. . . .

THE QUEEN: It's *my* image that ought to be there. . . .

THE ENVOY: You're already on the postage stamps, on the banknotes, on the seals in the police-stations.

THE GENERAL: The slowness of the carriage . . .

THE QUEEN: Will I therefore never be who I am?

THE ENVOY: Never again.

THE QUEEN: Every event of my life—my blood that trickles if I scratch myself. . . .

THE ENVOY: Everything will be written for you with a capital letter.

THE QUEEN: But that's Death?

THE ENVOY: It is indeed.

THE CHIEF OF POLICE (*with sudden authority*): It means death for all of you. And that's why I'm sure of you. At least, as long as I've not been impersonated, because after that I'll just sit back and take it easy. (*Inspired*) Besides, I'll know by a sudden weakness of my muscles that my image is escaping from me to go and haunt men's minds. When that happens my visible end will be near. For the time being, and if we have to act . . . (*To the Bishop*) who will assume real responsibilities? You? (*He shrugs.*) Be logical: if you are what you are, judge, general, bishop, it's because you wanted to become that and wanted it known that you had become it. You therefore did what was necessary to achieve your purpose and to be a focus of attention. Is that right?

THE JUDGE: Pretty much.

THE CHIEF OF POLICE: Very well. That means you've never performed an act for its own sake, but always so that, when linked with other acts, it would make a bishop, a judge, a general. . . .

THE BISHOP: That's both true and false. For each act contained within itself its leaven of novelty.

THE JUDGE: We acquired greater dignity thereby.

THE CHIEF OF POLICE: No doubt, my Lord, but this dignity, which has become as inhuman as a crystal, makes you unfit for governing men. No, no, gentlemen, above you, more sublime than you, is the Queen. It's from her, for the time being, that you derive your power and your rights. Above her—that to which she refers—is our standard, on which I've blazoned the image of Chantal Victorious, our saint.

THE BISHOP (*aggressively*): Above Her Majesty, whom we

venerate, and above her flag, is God, Who speaks through my voice.

THE CHIEF OF POLICE (*irritably*): And above God? (*A silence.*) Well, gentlemen, above God are you, without whom God would be nothing. And above you am I, without whom. . . .

THE JUDGE: What about the people? The photographers?

THE CHIEF OF POLICE: On their knees before the people who are on their knees before God. Therefore. . . .

(*They all burst out laughing.*)

That's why I want you to serve me. But a while ago you were holding forth quite volubly. I should therefore like to pay homage to your eloquence, your facility of elocution, the limpidity of your timbre, the potency of your organ. As for me, I'm a mere man of action who gets tangled up in words and ideas when they're not immediately applied. That's why I was wondering whether to send you back to your kennel. I won't do it. In any case, not right away, since you're already there.

THE GENERAL: Sir!

THE CHIEF OF POLICE (*He pushes the General, who topples over and remains sitting on the floor, flabbergasted*): Lie down! Lie down, General!

THE JUDGE: My skirt can be tucked up. . . .

THE CHIEF OF POLICE (*He pushes the Judge, who topples over*): Lie down! Since you want to be recognized as a judge, do you want to hold on to your dignity according to my idea of it? And according to the general meaning attached to your dignities? Very well. Must I therefore grant you increasing recognition along these lines? Yes or no? (*No one answers.*)

Well, gentlemen, yes or no? (THE BISHOP *steps aside, prudently.*)

THE QUEEN (*very blandly*): Excuse him, if he gets carried away. I'm quite aware of what you used to come here for: (*to the Bishop*) you, my Lord, to seek by quick, decisive ways a manifest saintliness. No, no, I'm not being ironic. The gold of my chasubles had little to do with it, I'm sure. It wasn't mere gross ambition that brought you behind my closed shutters. Love of God was hidden there. I realize that. You, my Lord, you were indeed guided by a concern for justice, since it was the image of a magistrate that you wished to see reflected a thousand times in my mirrors. And you, General, it was bravery and military glory and the heroic deed that haunted you. So let yourselves go, relax, without too many scruples. . . .

(*One after the other, the three men heave a deep sigh.*)

THE CHIEF OF POLICE (*continuing*): That's a relief to you, isn't it? You never really wanted to get out of yourselves and communicate, if only by acts of meanness, with the world. I understand you. (*Amiably*) My role, unfortunately, is in motion. In short, as you probably know, it's not in the nomenclature of the brothels. . . .

THE QUEEN: In the pink handbook.

THE CHIEF OF POLICE: Yes, in the pink handbook. (*To the Three Figures*) Come now, gentlemen, don't you feel sorry for a poor fellow like me? (*He looks at them one after the other.*) Come, come, gentlemen, you're not hardhearted, are you? It's for you that these Studios and Illustrious Rites were perfected, by means of exquisite experimentation. They required long labour, infinite patience, and you want to go back to the light of day? (*Almost humble, and suddenly looking very very tired*) Wait just a little while. For the time being, I'm still loaded with future acts, loaded with actions . . . but as soon as I feel I'm being multiplied ad infinitum, then . . . then, ceasing to be hard, I'll go and rot in people's minds. And you, get into your skirts again if you want to, and get back on the job. (*To* THE BISHOP) You're silent. (*A long silence.*) That's right. . . . Let's be silent, and let's wait. . . . (*A long and heavy silence.*) Perhaps it's now . . . (*In a low, humble voice*) that my apotheosis is being prepared. . . . (*Everybody is visibly expectant. Then,* CARMEN *enters, as if furtively, by the left door.* THE ENVOY *is the first to see her. He silently indicates her presence to* THE QUEEN. THE QUEEN *motions to* CARMEN *to withdraw, but* CARMEN *nevertheless takes a step forward.*)

84

THE QUEEN (*in an almost low voice*): I gave orders that we were not to be disturbed. What do you want?

(CARMEN *goes to her.*)

CARMEN: I tried to ring, but the apparatus is out of order. I beg your pardon. I'd like to speak with you.

THE QUEEN: Well, what is it? Speak up!

CARMEN (*hesitantly*): It's . . . I don't know. . . .

THE QUEEN (*resignedly*): Well, when at Court do as the Court does. Let's speak in an undertone. (*She conspicuously lends ear to* CARMEN, *who leans forward and murmurs a few words.* THE QUEEN *seems very upset.*)

THE QUEEN: Are you sure?

CARMEN: Quite, Madame.

(THE QUEEN *bolts from the room, followed by* CARMEN. THE CHIEF OF POLICE *starts to follow them, but the* ENVOY *intervenes.*)

THE ENVOY: One does not follow Her Majesty.

THE CHIEF OF POLICE: What's going on? Where's she going?

THE ENVOY (*ironically*): To embroider. The Queen is embroidering, and she is not embroidering. . . . You know the refrain? The Queen attains her reality when she withdraws, absents herself, or dies.

THE CHIEF OF POLICE: What's happening outside? (*To the Judge*) Do you have any news?

THE JUDGE: What you call outside is as mysterious to us as we are to it.

THE BISHOP: I shall try to depict the grief of this people which thought it had liberated itself by rebelling. A!as—or rather, thank Heaven!—there will never be a movement powerful enough to destroy our imagery.

THE CHIEF OF POLICE (*almost tremblingly*): So you think I have a chance?

THE BISHOP: You're in the best possible position. There's consternation everywhere, in all families, in all institutions. People have trembled so violently that your image is beginning to make them doubt themselves.

THE CHIEF OF POLICE: Am I their only hope?

THE BISHOP: Their only hope lies in utter collapse.

THE CHIEF OF POLICE: In short, I'm like a pool in which they behold themselves?

THE GENERAL (*delighted, with a burst of laughter*): And if they lean over too far, they fall in and drown. Before long, you'll be full of drowned bodies! (*No one seems to share his merriment.*) Oh well . . . they're not yet at the brink! (*Embarrassed*) Let's wait.
(*A silence.*)

THE CHIEF OF POLICE: So you really think the people had a wild hope? And that in losing all hope they lose everything? And that in losing everything they'll come and lose themselves in me? . . .

THE BISHOP: That may very well happen. But, believe me, not if we can help it.

THE CHIEF OF POLICE: When I am offered that final consecration. . . .

THE ENVOY (*ironically*): For you, but for you alone, for a second the Earth will stop rotating. . . .
(*Suddenly the door at the left opens and* THE QUEEN *appears, beaming.*)

THE QUEEN: George! (*She falls into the arms of the Chief of Police.*)

THE CHIEF OF POLICE (*incredulous*): It's not true. (THE QUEEN *nods yes.*) But where? . . . When?

THE QUEEN (*deeply moved*): There! . . . Now! The Studio. . . .

THE CHIEF OF POLICE: You're pulling my leg. I didn't hear anything.
(*Suddenly a tremendous ringing, a kind of peal of bells.*)
So it's true? It's for me? (*He pushes the Queen away. Solemnly, as the ringing stops:*) Gentlemen, I belong to the Nomenclature! (*To the Queen*) But are you really sure? (*The ringing starts again, then stops.*)

THE QUEEN: It was I who received him and ushered him into the Mausoleum Studio. The one that's being built in your honour. I left Carmen behind to attend to the preparations and I ran to let you know. I'm trembling like a leaf. . . .
(*The ringing starts again, then stops.*)

THE BISHOP (*gloomily*): We're up the creek.

86

THE CHIEF OF POLICE: The apparatus is working. You can see. . . .
  (*He goes to the left, followed by* THE QUEEN.)
THE ENVOY: That is not the practice. It's filthy. . . .
THE CHIEF OF POLICE (*shrugging his shoulders*): Where's the mechanism? (*To the Queen*) Let's watch together.
  (*She stands at the left, facing a small port-hole. After a brief hesitation,* THE JUDGE, GENERAL *and* BISHOP *place themselves at the right, at another port-hole symmetrical with the first. Then, the two panels of the double mirror forming the back of the stage silently draw apart, revealing the interior of the Special Studio.* THE ENVOY, *with resignation, joins the Chief of Police.*)

DESCRIPTION OF THE MAUSOLEUM STUDIO: *The stones of the wall, which is circular, are visible. At the rear, a stairway that descends. In the centre of this well there seems to be another, in which the steps of a stairway are visible. On the walls, four laurel wreaths, adorned with crêpe. When the panels separate,* ROGER *is at the middle of the stairway, which he is descending.* CARMEN *seems to be guiding him.* ROGER *is dressed like* THE CHIEF OF POLICE, *though, mounted on the same cothurni as the Three Figures, he looks taller. His shoulders have also been broadened. He descends the stairs to the rhythm of a drum.*

CARMEN (*approaching, and handing him a cigar*): It's on the house.
ROGER (*putting the cigar into his mouth*): Thanks.
CARMEN (*taking the cigar from him*): That end's for the light. This one's for the mouth. (*She turns the cigar around.*) Is this your first cigar?
ROGER: Yes. . . . (*A pause.*) I'm not asking for your advice. You're here to serve me, I've paid. . . .
CARMEN: I beg your pardon, sir.
ROGER: The slave?
CARMEN: He's being untied.
ROGER: He knows what it's about?
CARMEN: Completely. You're the first. You're inaugurating this Studio, but, you know, the scenarios are all reducible to a

87

major theme. . . .

ROGER: Which is. . . ?

CARMEN: Death.

ROGER (*touching the walls*): And so this is my tomb?

CARMEN (*correcting him*): Mausoleum.

ROGER: How many slaves are working on it?

CARMEN: The entire people, sir. Half of the population during the day and the other half at night. As you have requested, the whole mountain will be burrowed and tunnelled. The interior will have the complexity of a termite nest or of the Basilica of Lourdes—we don't know yet. No one will be able to see anything from the outside. All they'll know is that the mountain is sacred, but, inside, the tombs are already being enshrined in tombs, the cenotaphs in cenotaphs, the coffins in coffins, the urns. . . .

ROGER: What about here, where I am now?

CARMEN (*with a gesture of disdain*): An antechamber. An antechamber called the Valley of the Fallen. (*She mounts the underground stairway.*) In a little while, you'll go farther down.

ROGER: I'm not to hope to see the light of day again?

CARMEN: But . . . do you still want to?

(*A silence.*)

ROGER: It's really true that no one's ever been here before me?

CARMEN: In this . . . tomb, or in this . . . Studio?

(*A silence.*)

ROGER: Is everything really on right? My outfit? My toupet?

(THE CHIEF OF POLICE *turns to the Queen.*)

THE CHIEF OF POLICE: He knew I wear a toupet?

THE BISHOP (*snickering, to the Judge, and the General*): He's the only one who doesn't know that everyone knows it.

CARMEN (*to Roger*): Everything was carefully planned long ago. It's all been worked out. The rest is up to you.

ROGER (*anxiously*): You realize I'm feeling my way too. I've got to imagine what the Hero's like, and he's never shown himself much.

CARMEN: That's why we've taken you to the Mausoleum Studio. It's not possible to make many errors here, nor indulge your imagination.

(*A pause.*)

ROGER: Will I be alone?

CARMEN: Everything is padded. The doors are lined. So are the walls.

ROGER (*hesitantly*): What about . . . the mausoleum?

CARMEN (*forcefully*): Built into the rock. The proof is that there's water oozing from the walls. Deathly silent. As for light, the darkness is so thick that your eyes have developed astounding qualities. The cold? Yes, the coldness of death. It's been a gigantic job drilling through the mountain. Men are still groaning in order to hollow out a gigantic niche for you. Everything proves that you're loved and that you're a conqueror.

ROGER: Groaning? Could . . . could I hear the groaning?

(CARMEN *turns toward a hole dug out at the foot of the wall, from which emerges the head of the* BEGGAR, *the character seen in Scene 4. He is now the* SLAVE.)

CARMEN: Come here!

(THE SLAVE *crawls in.*)

ROGER (*looking the slave over*): Is that it?

CARMEN: A fine specimen, isn't he? Skinny. With lice and sores. He dreams of dying for you. I'll leave you alone now.

ROGER: With him? No, no. (*A pause.*) Stay. Everything always takes place in the presence of a woman. It's in order for a woman's face to be a witness that, usually. . . .

(*Suddenly, the sound of a hammer striking an anvil. Then a cock crows.*)

Is life so near?

CARMEN (*in a normal voice, not acting*): As I've told you, everything's padded, but some sounds always manage to filter through. Does it bother you? Life's starting up again little by little . . . as before. . . .

ROGER (*he seems anxious*): Yes, as before. . . .

CARMEN (*gently*): You were. . . .

ROGER: Yes. Everything's washed up. . . . And what's saddest of all is people's saying: "The rebellion was wonderful!"

CARMEN: You mustn't think about it any more. And you must

stop listening to the sounds from outside. Besides, it's raining. The whole mountain has been swept by a tornado. (*Stage voice*) You are at home here. (*Pointing to the slave*) Make him talk.

ROGER (*playing his role*): For you can talk? And what else can you do?

THE SLAVE (*lying on his belly*): First, bow; then, shrink into myself a little more (*He takes Roger's foot and places it on his own back.*) like this! . . . and even. . . .

ROGER (*impatiently*): Yes . . . and even?

THE SLAVE: Sink into the earth, if it's possible.

ROGER (*drawing on his cigar*): Sink in, really? But there's no mud?

THE QUEEN (*to the others*): He's right. We should have provided mud. In a well-run house. . . . But it's opening day, and he's the first client to use the Studio. . . .

THE SLAVE (*to Roger*): I feel it all over my body, sir. It's all over me, except in my mouth, which is open so that I can sing your praises and utter the groans that made me famous.

ROGER: Famous? You're famous, you?

THE SLAVE: Famous for my chants, sir, which are hymns to your glory.

ROGER: So your glory accompanies mine? (*To Carmen*) Does he mean that my reputation will be kept going by his words? And . . . if he says nothing, I'll cease to exist. . . ?

CARMEN (*curtly*): I'd like very much to satisfy you, but you ask questions that aren't in the scenario.

ROGER (*to the Slave*): But what about you, who sings to you?

THE SLAVE: Nobody. I'm dying.

ROGER: But without me, without my sweat, without my tears and blood, what would you be?

THE SLAVE: Nothing.

ROGER (*to the Slave*): You sing? But what else do you do?

THE SLAVE: We do all we possibly can to be more and more unworthy of you.

ROGER: What, for example?

THE SLAVE: We try hard just to stand and rot. And, believe me,

90

it's not always easy. Life tries to prevail. . . . But we stand our ground. We keep shrinking more and more every. . . .

ROGER: Day?

THE SLAVE: Week.

THE CHIEF OF POLICE (*to the others*): That's not much. With a little effort. . . .

THE ENVOY (*to the Chief of Police*): Be still. Let them play out their roles.

ROGER: That's not much. With a little effort. . . .

THE SLAVE (*with exaltation*): With joy, Your Excellency! You're so splendid! So splendid that I wonder whether you're aglow or whether you're all the darkness of all the nights?

ROGER: What does it matter, since I'm no longer to have any reality except in the reality of your phrases.

THE SLAVE (*crawling in the direction of the upper stairway*): You have not mouth nor ears nor eyes, but all of you is a thundering mouth and at the same time a dazzling and watchful eye. . . .

ROGER: *You* see it, but do the others know it? Does the night know it? Does death? Do the stones? What do the stones say?

THE SLAVE (*still dragging on his belly and beginning to crawl up the stairs*): The stones say. . . .

ROGER: Well, I'm listening.

THE SLAVE (*he stops crawling, and faces the audience*): The cement that holds us together to form your tomb. . . .

THE CHIEF OF POLICE (*facing the audience and joyfully beating his breast*): The stones venerate me!

THE SLAVE (*continuing*): . . . the cement is moulded of tears, spit and blood. The workers' eyes and hands that rested upon us have matted us with grief. We are yours, and only yours. (THE SLAVE *starts crawling up the stairs again.*)

ROGER (*with rising exaltation*): Everything proclaims me! Everything breathes me and everything worships me! My history was lived so that a glorious page might be written and then read. It's reading that counts. (*He suddenly notices that the Slave has disappeared. To Carmen*) But . . . where's he going? . . . Where is he? . . .

91

CARMEN: He's gone off to sing. He's going up into the light of day. He'll tell . . . that he carried your footsteps . . . and that. . . .

ROGER (*anxiously*): Yes, and that? What else will he tell?

CARMEN: The truth; that you're dead, or rather that you don't stop dying and that your image, like your name, reverberates to infinity.

ROGER: He knows that my image is everywhere?

CARMEN: Yes, everywhere, inscribed and engraved and imposed by fear.

ROGER: In the palms of stevedores? In the games of children? On the teeth of soldiers? In war?

CARMEN: Everywhere.

THE CHIEF OF POLICE (*to the others*): So I've made it?

THE QUEEN (*fondly*): Are you happy?

THE CHIEF OF POLICE: You've done a good job. That puts the finishing touch to your house.

ROGER (*To Carmen*): Is it in prisons? In the wrinkles of old people?

CARMEN: It is.

ROGER: In the curves of roads?

CARMEN: You mustn't ask the impossible.
(*Same sounds as earlier: the cock and the anvil.*)
It's time to go, sir. The session's over. Turn left, and when you reach the corridor. . . .
(*The sound of the anvil again, a little louder.*)
You hear? You've got to go home. . . . What are you doing?

ROGER: Life is nearby . . . and far away. Here all the women are beautiful. Their purpose is purely ornamental. . . . One can lose oneself in them. . . .

CARMEN (*curtly*): That's right. In ordinary language, we're called whores. But you've got to leave. . . .

ROGER: And go where? Into life? To carry on, as they say, with my activities. . . .

CARMEN (*a little anxiously*): I don't know what you're doing, and I haven't the right to inquire. But you've got to leave. Your time's up.

92

(The sound of the anvil and other sounds indicate an activity: cracking of a whip, humming of a motor, etc.)

ROGER: They give you the rush in this place! Why do you want me to go back where I came from?

CARMEN: You've nothing further to do. . . .

ROGER: There? No. Nothing further. Nor here either. And outside, in what you call life, everything has crashed. No truth was possible. . . . Did you know Chantal?

CARMEN *(suddenly frightened)*: Get going! Clear out of here!

THE QUEEN: I won't allow him to create a rumpus in my studios! Who was it who sent me that individual? Whenever there are disturbances, the riff-raff always crop up. I hope that Carmen. . . .

CARMEN *(to Roger)*: Get out! You've no right to ask questions either. You know that brothels are very strictly regulated and that we're protected by the police.

ROGER: No! Since I'm playing the Chief of Police and since you allow me to be here. . . .

CARMEN *(pulling him away)*: You're crazy! You wouldn't be the first who thought he'd risen to power. . . . Come along!

ROGER *(disengaging himself)*: If the brothel exists and if I've a right to go there, then I've a right to lead the character I've chosen to the very limit of his destiny . . . no, of mine . . . of merging his destiny with mine. . . .

CARMEN: Stop shouting, sir. All the studios are occupied. Come along. . . .

(CARMEN tries to make him leave. She opens a door, then another, then a third, unable to find the right one. ROGER takes out a knife and, with his back to the audience, makes the gesture of castrating himself.)

THE QUEEN: On my rugs! On the new carpet! He's a lunatic!

CARMEN *(crying out)*: Doing that here! *(She yells)* Madame! Mme Irma! *(CARMEN finally manages to drag Roger out.)*
(THE QUEEN rushes from the room. All the characters—the CHIEF OF POLICE, THE ENVOY, THE JUDGE, THE GENERAL, THE BISHOP—*turn and leave the port-holes.* THE CHIEF OF POLICE *moves forward to the middle of the stage.)*

THE CHIEF OF POLICE: Well played. He thought he had me.

(*He places his hand on his fly, very visibly feels his balls and, reassured, heaves a sigh.*) Mine are here. So which of us is washed up? He or I? Though my image be castrated in every brothel in the world, I remain intact. Intact, gentlemen. (*A pause.*) That plumber didn't know how to handle his role, that was all. (*He calls out, joyfully*) Irma! Irma! . . . Where is she? It's not her job to dress wounds.

THE QUEEN (*entering*): George! The vestibule . . . the rugs are covered with blood . . . the vestibule's full of clients. . . . We're wiping up as best we can. . . . Carmen doesn't know where to put them. . . .

THE ENVOY (*bowing to the Chief of Police*): Nice work.

THE CHIEF OF POLICE: An image of me will be perpetuated in secret. Mutilated? (*He shrugs his shoulders.*) Yet a low Mass will be said to my glory. Notify the kitchens! Have them send me enough grub for two thousand years.

THE QUEEN: What about me? George, *I'm* alive!

THE CHIEF OF POLICE (*without hearing her*): So. . . . I'm. . . . Where? Here, or . . . a thousand times there? (*He points to the tomb.*) Now I can be kind . . . and pious . . . and just. . . . Did you see? Did you see me? There, just before, larger than large, stronger than strong, deader than dead? So I've nothing more to do with you.

THE QUEEN: George! But I still love you!

THE CHIEF OF POLICE (*moving towards the tomb*): I've won the right to go and sit and wait for two thousand years. (*To the photographers*) You! Watch me live, and die. For posterity: shoot! (*Three almost simultaneous flashes.*) I've won! (*He walks backwards into the tomb, very slowly, while* THE THREE PHOTOGRAPHERS *casually leave by the left wing, with their cameras slung over their backs. They wave before disappearing.*)

THE QUEEN: But it was I who did everything, who organized everything. . . . Stay. . . . What will. . . .
(*Suddenly a burst of machine-gun fire.*)
You hear!

THE CHIEF OF POLICE (*with a burst of laughter*): Think of me!
(THE JUDGE *and* THE GENERAL *rush forward to stop him, but*
94

the doors start closing as the CHIEF OF POLICE *descends the first steps. A second burst of machine-gun fire.*)

THE JUDGE (*clinging to the door*): Don't leave us alone!

THE GENERAL (*gloomily*): That carriage again!

THE ENVOY (*to the Judge*): Be careful, you'll get your fingers caught.

(*The door has definitely closed. The characters remain bewildered for a moment. A third burst of machine-gun fire.*)

THE QUEEN: Gentlemen, you are free.

THE BISHOP: But . . . in the middle of the night?

THE QUEEN (*interrupting him*): You'll leave by the narrow door that leads into the alley. There's a car waiting for you.

(*She nods courteously. The Three Figures exeunt right. A fourth burst of machine-gun fire.*)

Who is it? . . . Our side? . . . Or rebels? . . . Or? . . .

THE ENVOY: Someone dreaming, Madame. . . .

(THE QUEEN *goes to various parts of the room and presses buttons. Each time, a light goes out.*)

THE QUEEN (*continuing to extinguish lights*): . . . Irma. . . . Call me Mme Irma and go home. Good night, sir.

THE ENVOY: Good night, Mme Irma.

(THE ENVOY *exits.*)

IRMA (*alone, and continuing to extinguish lights*): It took so much light . . . two pounds' worth of electricity a day! Thirty-eight studios! Every one of them gilded, and all of them rigged with machinery so as to be able to fit into and combine with each other. . . . And all these performances so that I can remain alone, mistress and assistant mistress of this house and of myself. (*She pushes in a button, then pushes it out again.*) Oh no, that's the tomb. He needs light, for two thousand years! . . . and food for two thousand years. . . . (*She shrugs her shoulders.*) Oh well, everything's in working order, and dishes have been prepared. Glory means descending into the grave with tons of victuals! . . . (*She calls out, facing the wings:*) Carmen? Carmen? . . . Bolt the doors, my dear, and put the furniture-covers on. . . . (*She continues extinguishing.*) In a little while, I'll have to start all over again . . . put all

95

the lights on again . . . dress up. . . . (*A cock crows.*) Dress up . . . ah, the disguises! Distribute roles again . . . assume my own. . . . (*She stops in the middle of the stage, facing the audience.*) . . . Prepare yours . . . judges, generals, bishops, chamberlains, rebels who allow the revolt to congeal, I'm going to prepare my costumes and studios for tomorrow. . . . You must now go home, where everything—you can be quite sure—will be falser than here. . . . You must go now. You'll leave by the right, through the alley. . . . (*She extinguishes the last light.*) It's morning already.

(*A burst of machine-gun fire.*)